EUGENE O'NEILL

Born in New York City in 1888, son of a well-known actor, Eugene O'Neill spent a year at Princeton University (1906) before signing on as a seaman and travelling widely. Following a period in a sanatorium recovering from TB, he wrote his first play, *A Wife for a Life*. In 1916 he joined the Provincetown Players, who produced the first of his plays to be staged, *Bound East for Cardiff*, as well as other early work. His Broadway debut came in 1920 with *Beyond the Horizon*, which also won him a Pulitzer Prize.

The next fourteen years saw the premieres of some twenty new plays, including *The Emperor Jones* (1920), *Anna Christie* (1921), which won a second Pulitzer Prize, *The Hairy Ape* (1922), *All God's Chillun Got Wings* (1924), *Desire Under the Elms* (1924), *The Great God Brown* (1926), *Strange Interlude* (1928), which won another Pulitzer, *Mourning Becomes Electra* (1931), a trilogy reworking the *Oresteia*, *Ah! Wilderness* (1933) and *Days Without End* (1933), after which thirteen years elapsed with no new play reaching the stage, though he continued writing. Two more plays were produced during his lifetime: *The Iceman Cometh* in 1946, though written in 1939, and *A Moon for the Misbegotten* in 1947, though it only reached Broadway ten years later, after his death in 1953.

Plays staged posthumously include *Long Day's Journey into Night* (1956), which won a fourth Pulitzer, *A Touch of the Poet* (1958) and *More Stately Mansions* (1962). He was three times married, his third wife, Carlotta Monterey, surviving him. In 1936 he became the first American dramatist to win the Nobel Prize for Literature.

EUGENE O'NEILL
DESIRE UNDER THE ELMS
&
THE GREAT GOD BROWN

Introduction by
Christine Dymkowski

ROYAL NATIONAL THEATRE
London

NICK HERN BOOKS

Desire Under the Elms & The Great God Brown first published in this edition in 1995 jointly by the Royal National Theatre, London and Nick Hern Books Limited, 14 Larden Road, London W3 7ST

Desire Under the Elms first published in Great Britain by Jonathan Cape in 1925
Copyright © 1924 by Eugene O'Neill

The Great God Brown first published in Great Britain by Jonathan Cape in 1926
Copyright © 1925 by Eugene O'Neill

Introduction Biographical Sketch of Eugene O'Neill and List of Produced Plays copyright © 1995 by Christine Dymkowski

Cover photograph of Eugene O'Neill by courtesy of the Raymond Mander & Joe Mitchenson Theatre Collection

Set by Seagull Books, Calcutta

Reprinted in 1999 by Athenæum Press Ltd, Gateshead, Tyne & Wear

British Library Cataloguing in Publication Data: a catalogue record for this book is available from the British Library

ISBN 1 85459 136 3

Contents

Biographical Sketch of Eugene O'Neill (1888–1953)

'Some day James O'Neill will best be known as the father of
Eugene O'Neill': so Eugene himself frequently boasted
throughout 1912. The claim struck those who heard it not with a
sense of the young man's prescience but of his presumption.
Nothing in his life so far had given any indication that in less
than a decade he would be a playwright to reckon with, shaking
up the American theatre and shaping a new American drama.
Instead, he seemed more likely to become one of the pipe-
dreamers who eternally inhabit Harry Hope's no-chance saloon in
his own *The Iceman Cometh*.

Born on 16 October 1888, to the respected and accomplished
actor James O'Neill and his wife Ella Quinlan O'Neill, Eugene
was to find his family an overwhelming force in his life and to
make it the almost constant subject of his plays. He was the
O'Neills' third son: the eldest, Jamie, had been born ten years
before; a second son, Edmund, had followed five years later. Life
was not easy for the O'Neills and their two young children; James
was already touring the country in *Monte Cristo*, the vehicle that
would spell both his financial success and his artistic defeat (he
succumbed to popular demand and played the role 4000 times
between 1883 and 1912). Ella, convent-educated and proper,
loved her husband but felt she had married beneath her; she
never took to James's theatrical life or to his theatrical friends.
However, the couple could not bear to be parted, and Ella, with
great reluctance, frequently left the children in the care of her
mother to join her husband on the road. Early in 1885, on one of
these occasions, Jamie contracted measles and disobeyed
instructions to stay away from his brother; Edmund became ill
and died.

Such family history might in another case seem irrelevant, but
it is crucial for an understanding of Eugene O'Neill and of his
work. Ella did not want any more children after Edmund's death,
but James, convinced that it would help solace her, persuaded
her to have another. The result was a family tragedy that
blighted all four lives, and not least the new baby, Eugene. In an
attempt to counteract the pain of an exceedingly difficult birth,
Ella was unwittingly precipitated into the morphine addiction

from which she would suffer for the next twenty-six years. James, Jamie, and Eugene were greatly affected by Ella's distraction and withdrawal from reality, but Jamie and Eugene endured a private hell of guilt: Jamie for inadvertently killing the brother whose loss had had such drastic consequences, and Eugene for having been born at all.

Fifteen when he learned of his mother's addiction, Eugene no longer had to fear the mental illness he had up till then suspected he would inherit; the truth, however, was worse. Although summers were spent at the family's home in New London, Connecticut, their haphazard existence in a succession of hotels while James was on tour had already given Eugene a sense of rootlessness that plagued him all his life. Now, guilty that his birth had effected such misery, he developed a deep sense of unbelonging that at times manifested itself as a death-wish. He rejected his parents' Catholicism and, under Jamie's influence, began to drink and to visit brothels. Both Jamie and Eugene, displacing their anger, blamed their father for their mother's condition, accusing him of hiring a 'quack' to attend Ella at Eugene's birth. In fact, even reputable doctors at that time prescribed morphine, and in doses so low that addiction was by no means inevitable.

Eugene entered Princeton in 1906, but only stayed a year, having spent most of his time drinking, cutting classes, and following his own reading interests. It was at this time that he discovered Nietzsche's *Thus Spake Zarathustra*, which together with the works of Strindberg, became his personal bible. After leaving Princeton, he worked for a short time in a New York office job arranged by his father. In the city's Greenwich Village, Hell's Kitchen, and Tenderloin districts, he began to frequent the dives he would immortalise in many of his plays and also began to write poetry. O'Neill remained a heavy drinker for years, though he never drank while writing; in 1926 he gave up alcohol completely, lapsing only a few times thereafter.

Wishing to escape from a romantic entanglement with Kathleen Jenkins, O'Neill let his father arrange for him to join a mining expedition in Honduras in October 1909. Nevertheless, because Kathleen was pregnant, he agreed to marry her shortly before his departure. Having contracted malaria after a few months in Central America, Eugene returned to the US and, without visiting his wife and new-born son (Eugene O'Neill, Jr.), joined his father's company on tour, checking tickets. Shortly afterwards, in June 1910, O'Neill boarded the *Charles Racine*, a Norwegian windjammer, as a working passenger on its two-month voyage to

Buenos Aires. O'Neill loved the sea – he was throughout his life a keen and able swimmer – and now had the chance to experience a sailing life first-hand; it was an experience he would exploit in many of his early plays.

O'Neill remained in Argentina for several months, occasionally working but mainly living as a down-and-out; he sailed back to New York in March 1911 on the S.S. *Ikala*, this time as a member of the crew. He stayed in New York long enough to arrange for a divorce, living in an alcoholic haze at a downtown bar and flophouse called Jimmy-the-Priest's. In July, he signed onto the S.S. *New York* as an ordinary seaman for its voyage to Southampton; he returned in August on the S.S. *Philadelphia* as an able-bodied seaman, a qualification of which he was to remain proud for the rest of his life. Resuming his destitute way of life at Jimmy-the-Priest's – though he regularly attended the performances of Dublin's Abbey Players, who were visiting New York – O'Neill sank progressively into a depression that in January 1912 culminated in a suicide attempt. When he had sufficiently recovered, he rejoined his father's company for a few months, this time taking on small acting roles.

1912 seemed to mark a watershed in O'Neill's life, as evidenced both by his boasting of future fame and by his setting of many of his most autobiographical plays in that year. Moving to New London, Connecticut, in the summer, he worked as a reporter for the *Telegraph*, continued to write poetry, and developed a mild case of tuberculosis. By the end of the year, he was at the Gaylord Farm Sanatorium, where he was to remain for six months. During that time he decided to become a playwright.

Returning to New London in summer 1913 and boarding with the Rippins, a local family, he began to write one-act plays based on his own experiences. O'Neill's father subsidised their publication as *Thirst and Other One Act Plays* in August 1914, and the following September O'Neill enrolled in Professor George Pierce Baker's famous play-writing course at Harvard. Although he did not particularly distinguish himself in the class, his disdain for easy formulaic success made clear his ambition to be an original dramatist.

After his year at Harvard, O'Neill returned to New York and became somewhat involved in the political and intellectual life of Greenwich Village, frequenting the Golden Swan saloon, familiarly known as the 'Hell Hole'. He submitted some plays to the adventurous Washington Square Players, who had recently formed in reaction to the glib, commercial offerings of Broadway; however, the Players were not so adventurous as to stage any of O'Neill's works.

His first real theatrical opportunity came in June 1916 when he accompanied his friend Terry Carlin to Provincetown, at the tip of Massachusetts's Cape Cod. Then, as now, Provincetown boasted a flourishing artists' colony each summer. The previous year, the writer Susan Glaspell, her husband Jig Cook, and other vacationing Greenwich Village friends had staged an impromptu production, marking the birth of what would become the Provincetown Players. When O'Neill arrived in Provincetown, the group were desperately short of plays for their new season. O'Neill offered them *Bound East for Cardiff*, which premiered on 28 July 1916, the first-ever performance of an O'Neill play. His work with the Players also led to his involvement in Greenwich Village's radical circle, which included John Reed, Louise Bryant, Mabel Dodge, and Floyd Dell, among others.

The Provincetown Players' success was such that in September 1916 they moved operations to Greenwich Village, acquiring a base on Macdougal Street, which at O'Neill's suggestion was named the Playwrights' Theatre. During the group's eight subscription seasons between 1916 and 1922, O'Neill had ample opportunity to experiment without regard to commercial considerations. For example, *The Emperor Jones*, staged by the Provincetown Players in November 1920, not only had an African-American for its protagonist but was also considerably shorter than standard length. Despite its unconventionality, the play marked the group's first popular success: following its scheduled performances at the Playwrights' Theatre, it moved uptown to Broadway for an unlimited run. When the original Provincetown Players disbanded, O'Neill, together with the designer Robert Edmond Jones and the critic-producer Kenneth Macgowan, founded the Experimental Theatre, Inc., in 1923. The triumvirate ran the Playwrights' Theatre, now renamed the Provincetown Playhouse, from 1923–25 and the Greenwich Village Theatre from 1924–26.

The Provincetown Players' success with *The Emperor Jones* was not O'Neill's first theatrical triumph. *Beyond the Horizon*, which opened at the Morosco Theatre on Broadway in February 1920, was greeted by extremely favourable reviews, transferred for an extended run, and brought O'Neill his first Pulitzer Prize (the second drama award in the prize's four-year history). This success was quickly followed by another: *Anna Christie* opened in November 1921 and brought him a second Pulitzer. He was to win the award twice more, for *Strange Interlude* in 1928 and posthumously in 1956 for *Long Day's Journey into Night*, a record that has not been matched.

By the time of his early success, O'Neill's personal life had
undergone considerable change: married for a second time, to
the writer Agnes Boulton, he had become a father again with the
birth of Shane Rudraighe O'Neill on 30 October 1919 (his last
child, Oona, who later married Charlie Chaplin, was born on 14
May 1925). His father had died in August 1920, having lived
long enough to see his younger son succeed; in the year prior to
his death, Eugene had finally recognised his father's long-
standing forbearance and support and had become friendly with
him. Ironically, O'Neill's own neediness so dominated his life that
he could never be a father to his own children, who all suffered
the neglect for which O'Neill had bitterly and unfairly resented
his own father. Eugene Jr. committed suicide at the age of forty,
and Shane was for many years a heroin addict.

Within three years of his father's death, O'Neill was the sole
survivor of his original family: his mother died of a brain tumour
in February 1922, and Jamie had drunk himself to death by
November 1923. Their deaths freed O'Neill to explore the dark
side of his family life, which he proceeded to do in plays as
diverse (and variously successful) as *All God's Chillun Got Wings*,
Dynamo, *Long Day's Journey into Night*, and *A Moon for the
Misbegotten*. Further change was in store: in 1927 O'Neill left
Agnes Boulton for Carlotta Monterey, who became his third wife
in July 1929. Misogynist, desirous of a mother, unable to separate
love from hate, O'Neill had difficult relationships with women.
He found his own guilt at his desertion of Agnes too difficult to
deal with, and, as he later did with his children, manufactured
grievances against her. His third marriage fulfilled his desire that
his wife should be completely dedicated to his own interests, but
it was a stormy one with cruelty on both sides.

O'Neill was quintessentially an autobiographical playwright:
many of his protagonists are recognisable O'Neill figures, sharing
the playwright's own lean build and dark deep-set eyes. All of his
experiences found their way onto the stage, from the sea-going
life depicted in early one-act plays like *Bound East for Cardiff* to
his ambivalence about parenthood in *The First Man* to his
Strindbergian view of marital relations in *Welded*. This need to
depict, explain, and justify himself had considerable ramifications
for his role as a playwright: he could not really regard theatre as
the collaborative activity it so patently is. Time and again. O'Neill
lamented the process of staging his plays, complaining that the
ideal play he had seen in his head never existed in production.
Whereas playwrights generally welcome the new life that actors

and directors bring to their work, O'Neill saw it as a betrayal. So strongly did he feel this that he virtually never went to any productions of his plays, only attending rehearsals in order to advise and to cut when necessary.

In addition, his personal investment in what he wrote often blinded him to its deficiencies: he could be convinced that inferior works like *Welded*, *Dynamo*, and *Days Without End* were undervalued and misjudged. For example, while *Dynamo* ostensibly focused on the relationship between humankind, machines, and religion, it was really O'Neill's working out of his ambivalent relationship to his mother: small wonder that it made more sense to O'Neill than to the critics. However, at his best, O'Neill was able to transmute his personal experiences into the most powerful of dramas, as he does in works like *Long Day's Journey into Night* and *The Iceman Cometh*.

Although he wrote essentially to please himself and to exorcise his private demons (as early as 1924 he claimed that 'Writing is my vacation from living'), O'Neill was genuinely interested in stretching American drama beyond the narrow confines it had so far inhabited. His experiments were many: trying to make the audience share a character's hallucination in *Where the Cross is Made*, extending the audience's endurance by writing four- and five-hour long plays, using set location schematically in *Beyond the Horizon*, incorporating expressionistic elements in *The Hairy Ape*, masking the characters in *The Great God Brown*, modernising the use of the aside in *Strange Interlude*, developing a modern equivalent for the Greek sense of tragedy in *Desire Under the Elms* and *Mourning Becomes Electra*, creating an ambitious play-cycle detailing a critical history of America through the story of one family in *A Tale of Possessors Self-Dispossessed* (of which only *A Touch of the Poet* was completed to his satisfaction).

Although his achievements won him the Nobel Prize for literature in 1936, in the last years of his life O'Neill was something of a has-been. He had suffered for years from a hand tremor, caused by a rare degenerative disease of the cerebellum that attacks the motor system, which made writing increasingly difficult; by 1943, it had become impossible. Since O'Neill had never been able to compose at a typewriter or by dictation, his writing career, apart from some revisions, was effectively over. Furthermore, he was extremely depressed by the Second World War: it made his writing seem of little consequence and the staging of his work even less important and appropriate. Consequently, he refused to authorise productions of new plays; none appeared between *Days Without End* in 1933 and *The Iceman*

Cometh in 1946. When the latter was finally staged, the inadequate production did little to restore interest in O'Neill's work.

Throughout his life, O'Neill had roamed far in search of a home and a sense of belonging: New York, Connecticut, Provincetown, Bermuda, France, Georgia, California. Sometime before his death on 27 November 1953, O'Neill struggled up from his bed to complain 'I knew it, I knew it! Born in a goddam hotel room and dying in a hotel room!' Only with the posthumous revival of *The Iceman Cometh* and the first production of *Long Day's Journey into Night* in 1956 did his reputation, like his life, come full circle.

Christine Dymkowski
Lecturer in Drama and Theatre Studies
Royal Holloway and Bedford New College
University of London

Introduction to the Plays

Following his brother Jamie's death on 8 November 1923, new creative energies were unleashed in O'Neill. Whether consciously or unconsciously, the playwright was freed to explore the raw experience of his family relationships and to shape it into two of his most powerfully-felt plays, *Desire Under the Elms* and *The Great God Brown*.

Both plays were developed in tandem. O'Neill began *Desire Under the Elms* on 15 January 1924 and worked on it for a fortnight, spending another week on it from 4–11 February before he was called away for rehearsals of *The Emperor Jones, All God's Chillun, Welded*, and his adaptation of *The Ancient Mariner*. On 23 April, he began work on *The Great God Brown*, an idea he had first recorded in his 1922 notebook. He outlined the plot on 29 April, and on 24 May turned again to *Desire*, finishing the first draft on 8 June. O'Neill then polished the play from 9–16 June and 1–2 July. After finishing *Marco Millions*, which he had begun in the summer of 1923, the playwright again turned his attention to *Brown*, working on it from 25 January to 25 March 1925 (Floyd, pp. 41–44, 54, 58, and Sheaffer, *Son & Artist*, p. 167).

In a letter written in 1945, O'Neill commented that he 'cannot explain at all' the origin either of *Desire Under the Elms* or of *Ah! Wilderness*: 'I had not the vestige of their idea in my notebook. I simply awakened with these plays in mind' (8/5/45 letter to Mr Maxwell, reprinted in Bogard & Bryer, p. 570). O'Neill had told his colleague Kenneth Macgowan the same story early in 1924; Macgowan, however, who had recently loaned him a copy of Sidney Howard's new play, *They Knew What They Wanted*, realised that O'Neill had unconsciously plagiarised its basic plot, which involves the young wife of an older farmer becoming pregnant by the foreman he treats as a son. Apart from this similarity, however, the two plays are very different, as Howard himself recognised: when *They Knew What They Wanted* won the Pulitzer Prize, its author felt the award should have gone to *Desire* (*Son & Artist*, pp. 126 & 160). It is easy to agree with Howard: the play's seamless blend of Greek tragedy, modern psychology, and O'Neill's own family history in a convincing American setting is a remarkable achievement.

The Greek origins of the play's concern with incest, infanticide, and father/son conflict, drawn from *Hippolytus* and *Medea* by Euripides and the Oedipus plays of Sophocles, have long been noted by O'Neill scholars. Sheaffer points out other sources in Wilhelm Stekel's book on sexual aberrations and in T. C. Murray's

Birthright, which O'Neill saw in an Abbey Players' production that
came to New York in 1911; its plot concerned 'a hard, unloving
Irishman who has developed "a cold, poor place" into a thriving
farm, his drudge of a wife, and their two sons, totally unlike one
another, who are rivals for the farm' (*Son & Artist*, pp. 121, 127–28).
Ranald also notes Nietzsche's continuing influence in Ephraim's
adherence to an 'Apollonian-Puritan God' and his occasional
succumbing to Dionysian impulses, an opposition O'Neill
developed much more strongly in *The Great God Brown* (pp. 175–76).

Although he was aware of his work and even read *Beyond the
Pleasure Principle* and *Group Psychology and the Analysis of the Ego* as he
wrote *Brown* in early 1925 (Work Diary, Floyd, p. 74), O'Neill always
denied Freud was a conscious influence. In response to a question
about its bearing on *Desire*, he insisted that 'Whatever of
Freudianism is in [it] must have walked right in "through my
unconscious"' (5/2/25 letter to Mr. Perlman, reprinted in Bogard
& Bryer, p. 192). Although O'Neill is often disingenuous about the
sources of his work, the autobiographical nature of *Desire Under the
Elms* suggests that perhaps here he was telling the truth: the
psychological and inter-generational conflicts of the play reflect his
own experience as much as they do Freudian theory. The myriad
correspondences between *Desire* and the playwright's own life have
been pointed out by his biographers, most perceptively by Sheaffer.
The Cabot farm with its elms gloomily hugging the house
resembles the Monte Cristo cottage in New London, as well as a
farm near O'Neill's adult Connecticut home. The playwright's
conscious attitudes to his parents are reflected in the portraits of
Ephraim and Eben: both Ephraim's meanness and his conflicts
with his sons embody O'Neill's view of his father, while Eben's
feelings for his mother mirror those of O'Neill toward his own.
However, many of Ephraim's traits depict the playwright himself:
his scorn for anything 'easy', his failures as father and husband, his
sense of being isolated and misunderstood (*Son & Artist*, pp.
129–30). O'Neill himself proclaimed his connection to the
character: 'I always have loved Ephraim so much! He's so
autobiographical!' (quoted in *Son & Artist*, p. 130).

The Great God Brown has similar roots: its sources lie in the
playwright's reading of Freud and Nietzsche, in his friend Edward
Keefe's failure as an artist and resort to architecture, and in his wife
Agnes Boulton's dream that O'Neill had returned home as a
different person (*Son & Artist*, pp. 170–71). Like most of his plays,
it is also deeply autobiographical, with preoccupations that are
echoed throughout his work: it is concerned, like his first full-
length drama, the unpublished and unproduced 'Bread and
Butter', 'with a failed artist, crucified by life and imprisoned in
marriage, who takes refuge in self-induced death' (*Son & Artist*, p.
168). Even more significantly, however, *The Great God Brown* looks
forward to O'Neill's emotional exorcism of private demons in his

last two full-length plays, *Long Day's Journey into Night* and *A Moon for the Misbegotten*.

O'Neill's diary relates that he finished the play, which remained one of his personal favourites, 'in tears! Couldn't control myself!' (quoted in *Son & Artist*, p. 167); its composition was as emotionally harrowing an experience as the writing of *Long Day's Journey*, from which he would emerge 'gaunt and sometimes weeping' (Carlotta Monterey, quoted in *Son & Artist*, p. 505). Dion Anthony, like so many of O'Neill's heroes, is a self-portrait in terms both of temperament and of looks: '*lean and wiry, . . .[with a face] dark, spiritual, poetic, passionately supersensitive*' (Prologue stage directions). However, he is at the same time a portrait of O'Neill's brother Jamie. Dion's '*defiant and mocking*' mask, which becomes more and more '*Mephistophelean*' [sic] as the play progresses (I. 1. stage directions), links him to the Jamie Tyrone of both the late plays: in *Long Day's Journey* Jamie's '*habitual expression of cynicism . . . gives his countenance a Mephistophelian cast*' (I. stage directions), while in *Moon for the Misbegotten* '*a certain Mephistophelian quality. . . is accentuated by his habitually cynical expression*' (I. stage directions). The implications of this dual portrait are spelled out more clearly in *Long Day's Journey* when Jamie confronts his brother: 'I've had more to do with bringing you up than anyone. . . Hell, you're more than my brother. I made you! You're my Frankenstein!' (IV). In *The Great God Brown*, O'Neill seems to be struggling to define his own self, just as, towards the close of the play, William Brown frenetically slips between his own mask and Dion's.

The use of masks in the play constitutes one of its greatest challenges and difficulties. O'Neill had become interested in the potential of masks when Blanche Hayes, the designer for *The Hairy Ape*, introduced them to fulfil a stage direction for uniform characters; O'Neill's life-long distrust of actors may have further enhanced their appeal. In *The Great God Brown*, O'Neill extended their symbolism, using them to represent the dichotomy between the internal and the social selves. For example, Dion wears a mask to hide his raw self from those around him; only with Cybel (a pure 'impure' woman, like Josie Hogan in *Moon for the Misbegotten*) can he be himself, maskless. More confusingly, however, Dion's mask also symbolises a transferable personality: after Dion's death, Brown assumes his mask and thereby his identity as Margaret's husband (in fact, O'Neill had originally hoped that the same actor who played Dion would play Brown in the second half of the play). Not only does the convention established at the play's beginning simply dissolve at this point, but O'Neill's careful grounding of the action in realistic detail makes it doubly difficult for an audience to accept such a transfer of the mask in comprehensible terms. Indeed, towards the end of the play, Brown's mask is even more problematically brought on stage by two men as if it were a body being carried by its legs and shoulders (IV. 1. stage directions).

Desire Under the Elms was the first O'Neill production at the Greenwich Village Theatre, which the Triumvirate of Experimental Theatre, Inc., rented for its second season, in addition to the smaller Provincetown Theatre (Wainscott, p. 157); it opened on 11 November 1924. Although the play was directed and designed by Robert Edmond Jones, O'Neill had in fact himself designed the basic set, which Jones simply modified, making it into 'a more attractive stage picture, yet a more severe homestead' (Wainscott. p. 161). Although Wainscott judges the appearance of the elms impressive in extant photographs, O'Neill was dissatisfied with them: in a letter to Macgowan, he complained that 'There have never been the elm trees of my play, characters almost' (letter written after 12/8/26, reprinted in Bryer, p. 132). On the other hand, O'Neill was delighted with Walter Huston's performance as Ephraim. A vaudeville player who had previously done little serious acting, Huston was critically acclaimed in the part. He also earned O'Neill's highest accolade, that of having realised the playwright's conception of the character. Huston was one of only three actors to achieve such praise, the others being Charles Gilpin in *The Emperor Jones* and Louis Wolheim in *The Hairy Ape*.

The play itself had mixed reviews, many critics expressing distaste for its subject matter. Nevertheless, it proved a popular success, playing at the 300–seat Greenwich Village Theatre for two months before transferring to Broadway, where it played at a succession of theatres. It first moved to the Earl Carroll on 12 January 1925, then to the smaller George M. Cohan on 1 June, and finally to Daly's 63rd Street on 28 September, where it played until 17 October 1925, for a total of 208 performances. The production grossed $395,000, making it O'Neill's greatest success to date (Miller, pp. 59–60; *Son & Artist*, p. 160). The popularity of *Desire Under the Elms* was no doubt enhanced by its notoriety: shortly after its move to Broadway, the New York district attorney attempted to have the play banned as immoral. Although he failed when the play was acquitted by a play-jury, *Desire* was not only successfully banned in Boston, but its road company was arrested in Los Angeles. The cast had to give a special performance of the play for the court and, although they received four curtain calls, the jury was split eight to four in favour of conviction; the judge had to dismiss them and order a retrial (Seiler, pp. 446–47).

The Great God Brown was the last O'Neill play to be staged by Experimental Theatre, Inc. Again directed and designed by Jones, it opened at the Greenwich Village Theatre on 23 January 1926. Although O'Neill's inconsistent use of masks caused much confusion, critical response to the play was generally positive, with reviewers admiring its ambitious scope and experimental nature. Interestingly, one of the reviews suggests Macgowan's claim in th programme notes that O'Neill's play was 'the first in which mask have ever been used to dramatise changes and conflicts in character' was not entirely justified; Alexander Woollcott remarked that 'the mask device . . . grows wearisome when so stuntful a scheme is prolonged any further than it was in . . . "Overtones"' (*World*, 25/1/26). This one-act play by Alice Gerstenberg, which had been produced by the Washington Square Players in 1915, 'used the Freudian concepts of ego and id to project the divided selves of her two characters. Each woman is shadowed by a veiled alter ego who speaks her innermost feelings in . . . [what] is thought to be the first American play "to depart from realism to show the unconscious"' (Introduction, Chinoy & Jenkins, p. 6).

The masks used in Jones's production, which had been designed by James Light and William Stahl, did not fulfil O'Neill's stage directions, which called for changes in the masks' appearance as the play progressed; lack of time meant that each actor had only one mask (Wainscott, p. 191). O'Neill later complained that because these masks merely conveyed the notion of 'hypocritical and defensive double-personality', they became 'an unnecessary trick' that failed to convey his true meaning (letter to Benjamin de Casseres, 22/6/27, reprinted in Bogard & Bryer, p. 246). In faet, O'Neill's meaning is so convoluted as to defy comprehension, irrespective of the number and type of masks used. The understandably mystified response to *The Great God Brown* when it first opened prompted the playwright to write to several New York newspapers to explain, unsuccessfully, its meaning. He pointed out the symbolism of Dion Anthony's name: the character embodies the Dionysian 'creative pagan acceptance of life, fighting eternal war with the masochistic, life-denying spirit of Christianity as represented by St. Anthony'. Margaret is a 'modern direct descendant' of Faust's Marguerite, 'the eternal girl-woman . . . properly oblivious to everything but the means to her end of maintaining the race', while Cybel is 'the Earth Mother' regarded as a 'pariah in a world of unnatural laws'. Brown himself represents 'Success', 'the visionless demi-god of our new materialistic myth'. However, O'Neill stressed that

> This background pattern of conflicting tides in the soul of Man should [n]ever overshadow and thus throw out of proportion the living drama of the recognisable human beings, Dion, Brown, Margaret and Cybel.
>
> I meant it always to be mystically within and behind them, giving them a significance beyond themselves, forcing itself through them to its expression in mysterious words, symbols, actions they do not themselves comprehend. And that is as clearly as I wish an audience to comprehend it (Post, 13/2/26).

Both in these final lines and in his summation of the play as a 'mystery' that can be felt but not understood, O'Neill implicitly admits the failure of his exegesis.

In fact, O'Neill's attempt to explain the play illuminates its failings. Grafting painful autobiographical material onto a seemingly neat but ultimately confused framework, *The Great God Brown* fails to cohere either as symbolic or as realistic drama. Margaret and Cybel, far from being 'recognisable human beings', reflect O'Neill's troubled attitude towards women, their sexuality, and his possible relationship with them: his greatest desire was for a mother-substitute who would suppress every personal need in order to fulfil his own. In contrast, Brown and Dion come fitfully to life throughout the play, not as their own individual selves but as embodiments of their creator's own struggle with existence. Dion Anthony's cry of despair — 'why the devil was I ever born at all?' — echoes resoundingly throughout O'Neill's work. *He* is the recognisable human being at the heart of *The Great God Brown*, and his existential pain gives the play, despite its manifest flaws, an undeniable power.

This power was certainly recognised by the audiences who flocked to the first production; after playing for five weeks at the small Greenwich Village Theatre, the production transferred to the 500-seat Garrick on 1 March and then to the 800-seat Klaw on 10 May, where it ran for about six months for a total run of 283 performances (Miller, p. 61; *Son & Artist*, pp. 194–95). The production grossed $193,000, making it, after *Desire Under the Elms*, the Triumvirate's second greatest financial success.

Both plays were first seen in London in private performances directed by Peter Godfrey. Presumably because its experimental nature gave it only a minority appeal, *The Great God Brown* opened in a Stage Society production at the Strand Theatre on 20 June 1927; John Gielgud played Dion Anthony and Oliver Messel designed the masks. Although the expressionist production and its acting were praised, the play had a mixed critical reception: St. John Ervine found 'moments of great beauty' and 'lyric loveliness' in a play giving merely 'a few elementary facts about elementary psychology'; James Agate regarded the 'second half . . . not only impossible of realisation, but . . . patently absurd' (Theatre Museum clippings). Because it had been banned for immorality by the Lord Chamberlain, *Desire Under the Elms* opened at the Gate, a private theatre club founded by Godfrey, on 24 February 1931; Normal Marshall's account of the production praises Eric Portman's 'fine performance' as Eben and judges the then-unknown Flora Robson's portrayal of Abbie as 'the finest [she] has ever given' (p. 48).

Desire Under the Elms has had notable revivals both in New York and in London. After it was finally granted a licence by the Lord Chamberlain in November 1938, *Desire* opened at the Westminster Theatre, London, on 24 January 1940, directed by Michael Macowan, with Beatric Lehmann as Abbie and Mark Dignam as Ephraim. It was most recently seen in London in a powerful staging by Patrick Mason at Greenwich Theatre, which opened on 11 May

1987 with Tom Hickey as Ephraim, Colin Firth as Eben, and Carmen du Sautoy as Abbie. Its first Broadway revival was on 16 January 1952 at the ANTA Playhouse; directed by Harold Clurman and starring Karl Malden as Ephraim, the production was originally scheduled for a two-week run but was extended for a further four, for a total of 46 performances. Both the play and the production, particularly Malden's performance, were highly praised. *Desire* was subsequently revived by José Quintero at the Circle-in-the-Square on 8 January 1963, with Rip Torn as Eben, George C. Scott as Ephraim, and Colleen Dewhurst as Abbie. Although there was critical disagreement about the effectiveness of Quintero's staging of the play on different levels on an arena stage, the production proved a huge popular success, running for 384 performances.

The Great God Brown, understandably, has not proved so popular with audiences. It was first revived in 1959 by New York's Phoenix Theatre under the direction of Stuart Vaughan; opening at the Coronet Theatre on 6 October, with Robert Lansing as Brown and Fritz Weaver as Anthony, it played for 32 subscription performances. The play was next staged in New York at the Lyceum Theatre on 10 December 1972, directed by Harold Prince for a limited run of 19 performances by the New Phoenix Repertory Company. *Brown* has received only one further British production since it was first seen in London; directed by Michael Walling and designed by Maria-Luise Walek for Stage One, it played at London's Rudolph Steiner Theatre from 8–26 September 1992 and then toured nationally from 29 September to 28 November. Despite its rarity value, the play received scant critical attention.

Christine Dymkowski
November 1993

Sources

Bogard, Travis and Jackson R. Bryer, eds. *Selected Letters of Eugene O'Neill.* New Haven and London: Yale University Press, 1988.

Bryer, Jackson R., ed. '*The Theatre We Worked For': The Letters of Eugene O'Neill to Kenneth Macgowan.* New Haven and London: Yale University Press, 1982.

Cargill, Oscar, et al., eds. *O'Neill and His Plays: Four Decades of Criticism.* New York: New York University Press, 1961.

Chinoy, Helen Crich and Linda Walsh Jenkins, eds. *Women in American Theatre.* Revised edition. New York: Theatre Communications Group, 1987.

Floyd, Virginia, ed. *Eugene O'Neill at Work: Newly Released Ideas for Plays.* New York: Frederick Ungar, 1981.

Gelb, Arthur and Barbara. *O'Neill.* New York: Harper, 1960.

Marshall, Norman. *The Other Theatre.* London: John Lehmann, 1947.

Miller, Jordan Y. *Eugene O'Neill and the American Critic: A Summary and Bibliographical Checklist.* Second edition, revised. Hamden, Connecticut: Archon, 1973.

Ranald, Margaret Loftus. *The Eugene O'Neill Companion.* Westport, Connecticut, and London: Greenwood, 1984.

Seiler, Conrad. 'Los Angeles Must Be Kept Pure', *The Nation*, 19 May 1926, reprinted in Cargill, pp. 443–48.

Sheaffer, Louis. *O'Neill: Son and Playwright.* London: Dent, 1968.
—————— . *O'Neill: Son and Artist.* London: Paul Elek, 1973.

Wainscott, Ronald H. *Staging O'Neill: The Experimental years, 1920–1934.* New Haven and London: Yale University Press, 1988.

I am extremely grateful to Sue Cusworth of Royal Holloway, University of London, for generously sharing research material collected for her doctoral dissertation on the importance of scenography in the work of O'Neill.

List of O'Neill's Produced Plays

Title	Year Written*	First Production	First London Production
The Web	1913–14	39th Street Theatre, New York 17 March 1924	
Thirst	1913–14	Wharf Theatre, Provincetown, Mass. Summer 1916	
Fog	1913–14	Playwrights' Theater, New York 5 January 1917	
Bound East for Cardiff	1913–14	Wharf Theatre, Provincetown, Mass. 28 July 1916	(see *S.S. Glencairn*)
Servitude	1913–14	Skylark Theatre N.Y. International Airport 22 April 1960	
Abortion	1913–14	Key Theatre, New York 27 October 1959	
The Movie Man	1914	Key Theatre, New York 27 October 1959	

The Sniper	1915	Playwright's Theater, New York 16 February 1917	Gate Theatre 30 August 1926
Before Breakfast	1916	Playwrights' Theater, New York 1 December 1916	Everyman Theatre 17 April 1922
Ile	1916–17	Playwrights' Theater, New York 30 November 1917	Everyman Theatre 15 June 1921
In the Zone	1916–17	Comedy Theater, New York (Washington Square Players) 31 October 1917	
The Long Voyage Home	1916–17	Playwrights' Theater, New York 2 November 1917	Everyman Theatre 12 June 1925
The Moon of The Caribbees	1916–17	Playwrights' Theater, New York 20 December 1918	(see *S.S. Glencairn*)
S.S. Glencairn (*Bound East for Cardiff, In the Zone, Moon of the Caribbees, and Long Voyage Home*)		Barnstormer's Barn Provincetown, Massachusetts 14 August 1924	Mercury Theatre 9 June 1947
The Rope	1918	Playwrights' Theater, New York 26 April 1918	

Title	Year Written*	First Production	First London Production
The Dreamy Kid	1918	Playwrights' Theater, New York 31 October 1919	(Festival Theatre, Cambridge 14 May 1928)
Beyond the Horizon	1918	Morosco Theater, New York 3 February 1920	Regent Theatre (The Repertory Players) 31 January 1926
Where the Cross is Made	1918	Playwrights' Theater, New York 22 November 1918	Arts Theatre 27 October 1927
The Straw	1918–19	Greenwich Village Theater, New York 10 November 1921 (after an out-of-town try-out)	
Exorcism	1919	Playwrights' Theater, New York 26 March 1920	
Chris (1st version of Anna Christie)	1919	Apollo Theater, Atlantic City, N.J. 8 March 1920	
Gold	1920	Frazee Theater, New York 1 June 1921	

Anna Christie	1920	Vanderbilt Theater, New York 2 November 1921	Strand Theatre 10 April 1923
The Emperor Jones	1920	Playwrights' Theater, New York 1 November 1920	Ambassadors' Theatre 10 September 1925
Diff'rent	1920	Playwrights' Theater, New York 27 December 1920	Everyman Theatre 4 October 1921
The First Man	1921	Neighborhood Playhouse, New York 4 March 1922	
The Hairy Ape	1921	Playwrights' Theater, New York 9 March 1922	Gate Theatre 26 January 1928
The Fountain	1921–22	Greenwich Village Theater, New York 10 December 1925	
Welded	1922–23	39th Street Theater, New York 17 March 1924	The Playroom Six 16 February 1928
All God's Chillun Got Wings	1923	Provincetown Playhouse, New York 15 May 1924	Gate Theatre 8 November 1926
The Ancient Mariner (adaptation)	1924	Provincetown Playhouse (previously Playwrights' Theater), New York 6 April 1924	

Title	Year Written*	First Production	First London Production
Desire Under The Elms	1924	Greenwich Village Theater, New York 11 November 1924	Gate Theatre 24 February 1931
Marco Millions	1923–25	Guild Theater, New York 9 January 1928	Westminster Theatre 26 December 1938 (also produced at Festival Theatre, Cambridge, 1932)
The Great God Brown	1925	Greenwich Village Theater, New York 23 January 1926	Strand Theatre (Stage Society) 19 June 1927
Lazarus Laughed	1925–26	Pasadena Community Playhouse, California 9 April 1928	
Strange Interlude	1926–27	John Golden Theater, New York 30 January 1928	Lyric Theatre 3 February 1931
Dynamo	1928	Martin Beck Theater, New York 11 February 1929	
Mourning Becomes Electra	1929–31	Guild Theater, New York 26 October 1931	Westminster Theatre 19 November 1937

Ah! Wilderness	1932	Nixon Theater, Pittsburgh, Pennsylvania 25 September 1933 (out-of-town tryout before New York opening at Guild Theater, 2 October 1933)	Westminster Theatre 4 May 1936
Days Without End	1932–33	Plymouth Theater, Boston, Mass. 27 December 1933 (out-of-town tryout before New York opening at Guild Theater, 8 January 1934)	Grafton Theatre (Stage Society) 3 February 1935
A Touch of the Poet	1935–42	Royal Dramatic Theatre, Stockholm, Sweden 29 March 1957 (first American production at Helen Hayes Theater, New York, 2 October 1958)	Young Vic Theatre 20 January 1988 (also produced at Ashcroft Theatre, Croydon, 16 September 1963)
More Stately Mansions	1936–42	Royal Dramatic Theatre, Stockholm, Sweden 11 September 1962 (first American production at Ahmanson Theater, Los Angeles, California, 12 November 1967)	Greenwich Theatre 19 September 1974
The Iceman Cometh	1939	Martin Beck Theater, New York 9 October 1946	Arts Theatre 29 January 1958

Title	Year Written*	First Production	First London Production
Long Day's Journey into Night	1939–41	Royal Dramatic Theatre, Stockholm, Sweden 10 February 1956 (first American production at Helen Hayes Theater, New York, 7 November 1956)	Globe Theatre 24 September 1958 (transfer from Lyceum Theatre, Edinburgh, 8 September 1958)
Hughie	1941–42	Royal Dramatic Theatre, Stockholm, Sweden 18 September 1958	Duchess Theatre 18 June 1963
A Moon for the Misbegotten	1943	Hartman Theater, Coiumbus, Ohio (Guild Theater production) 20 February 1947	Arts Theatre 20 January 1960

*Dates of composition are approximate.

DESIRE UNDER THE ELMS

A Play in Three Parts

Characters

EPHRAIM CABOT
SIMEON ⎤
PETER ⎬ His Sons
EBEN ⎦
ABBIE PUTNAM
Young Girl, Two Farmers, The Fiddler, A Sheriff, And Other
People From The Surrounding Farms

General Scene

The action of the entire play takes place in, and immediately outside of, the Cabot farm-house in New England, in the year 1850. The south end of the house faces a stone wall with a wooden gate at centre opening on a country road. The house is in good condition, but in need of paint. Its walls are a sickly greyish, the green of the shutters faded. Two enormous elms are on each side of the house. They bend their trailing branches down over the roof – they appear to protect and at the same time subdue; there is a sinister maternity in their aspect, a crushing, jealous absorption. When the wind does not keep them astir, they develop from their intimate contact with the life of man in the house an appalling humaneness. They brood oppressively over the house, they are like exhausted women resting their sagging breasts and hands and hair on its roof, and when it rains their tears trickle down monotonously and rot on the shingles.

There is a path running from the gate around the right corner of the house to the front door. A narrow porch is on this side. The end wall facing us has two windows in its upper storey, two larger ones on the floor below. The two upper are those of the father's bedroom and that of the brothers. On the left, ground floor, is the kitchen – on the right, the parlour, the blinds of which are always pulled down.

PART ONE

Scene One

*Exterior of the Farm-house. It is sunset of a day at the beginning of summer
in the year 1850. There is no wind and everything is still. The sky above the
roof is suffused with deep colours, the green of the elms glows, but the house
is in shadow, seeming pale and washed out by contrast.*

A door opens and EBEN CABOT *comes to the end of the porch and stands
looking down the road to the right. He has a large bell in his hand and this
he swings mechanically, awakening a deafening clangour. Then he puts his
hands on his hips and stares up at the sky. He sighs with a puzzled awe
and blurts out with halting appreciation.*

EBEN. God! Purty!

*His eyes fall and he stares about him frowningly. He is twenty-five, tall
and sinewy. His face is well formed, good-looking, but its expression is
resentful and defensive. His defiant dark eyes remind one of a wild
animal's in captivity. Each day is a cage in which he finds himself
trapped, but inwardly unsubdued. There is a fierce repressed vitality
about him. He has black hair, moustache, a thin curly trace of beard.
He is dressed in rough farm clothes.*

*He spits on the ground with intense disgust, turns and goes back into
the house.*

SIMEON *and* PETER *come in from their work in the fields. They are
tall men, much older than their half-brother (*SIMEON *is thirty-nine
and* PETER *thirty-seven), built on a squarer, simpler model, fleshier in
body, more bovine and homelier in face, shrewder and more practical.
Their shoulders stoop a bit from years of farm work. They clump heavily
along in their clumsy thick-soled boots caked with earth. Their clothes,
their faces, hands, bare arms and throats are earth-stained. They smell
of earth. They stand together for a moment in front of the house and, as
if with the one impulse, stare dumbly up at the sky, leaning on their
hoes. Their faces have a compressed, unresigned expression. As they look
upward, this softens.*

SIMEON *(grudgingly)*. Purty.

PETER. Ay-eh.

SIMEON *(suddenly)*. Eighteen year ago.

PETER. What?

SIMEON. Jenn. My woman. She died.

PETER. I'd fergot.

SIMEON. I rec'lect – now an' agin. Makes it lonesome. She'd hair long's a hoss's tail – an' yaller like gold!

PETER. Waal – she's gone (*This with indifferent finality – then after a pause.*) They's gold in the West, Sim.

SIMEON (*still under the influence of sunset – vaguely*). In the sky?

PETER. Waal – in a manner o'speakin' – thar's the promise. (*Growing excited.*) Gold in the sky – in the west – Golden Gate – Californi-a! – Golden West! – fields o'gold!

SIMEON (*excited in his turn*). Fortunes layin' just atop o' the ground waitin' t' be picked! Solomon's mines they says! (*For a moment they continue looking up at the sky — then their eyes drop.*)

PETER (*with sardonic bitterness*). Here – it's stones atop o' the ground - stones atop o' stones – makin' stone walls – year atop o' year – him 'n' yew 'n' me 'n' then Eben – makin' stone walls fur him to fence us in.

SIMEON. We've wuked. Give our strength. Give our years. Ploughed 'em under in the ground (*He stamps rebelliously.*) – rottin' – makin' soil for his crops! (*A pause.*) Waal – the farm pays good for hereabouts.

PETER. If we ploughed in Californi-a, they'd be lumps o' gold in the furrow –!

SIMEON. Californi-a's t'other side o' earth, a'most. We got t' calc'late –

PETER (*after a pause*). 'Twould be hard fur me, too, to give up what we've 'arned here by our sweat. (*A pause. EBEN sticks his head out of the dining-room window, listening.*)

SIMEON. Ay-eh. (*A pause.*) Mebbe – he'll die soon.

PETER (*doubtfully*). Mebbe.

SIMEON. Mebbe – fur all we knows – he's dead now.

PETER. Ye' need proof –

SIMEON. He's been gone two months – with no word.

PETER. Left us in the fields an evenin' like this. Hitched up an' druv off into the West. That's plumb onnateral. He hain't never been off this farm 'ceptin' t' the village in thirty year or more, not since he married Eben's maw. (*A pause. Shrewdly.*) I calc'late we might git him declared crazy by the court.

SIMEON. He skinned 'em too slick. He got the best o' all on 'em. They'd never b'lieve him crazy. (*A pause.*) We got t' wait– till he's under ground.

EBEN (*with a sardonic chuckle*). Honour thy father! (*They turn startled and stare at him. He grins, then scowls.*) I pray he's died. (*They stare at him. He continues matter-of-factly.*) Supper's ready.

SIMEON *and* PETER (*together*). Ay-eh.

EBEN (*gazing up at the sky*). Sun's downin' purty.

SIMEON *and* PETER (*together*). Ay-eh. They's gold in the West.

EBEN. Ay-eh. (*Pointing.*) Yonder atop o' the hill pasture, ye mean?

SIMEON *and* PETER (*together*). In Californi-a!

EBEN. Hunh? (*Stares at them indifferently for a second, then drawls.*) Waal – supper's gittin' cold. (*He turns back into kitchen.*)

SIMEON (*startled – smacks his lips*). I air hungry!

PETER (*sniffing*). I smells bacon!

SIMEON (*with hungry appreciation*). Bacon's good!

PETER (*in the same tone*). Bacon's bacon!

They turn, shouldering each other, their bodies bumping and rubbing together as they hurry clumsily to their food, like two friendly oxen toward their evening meal. They disappear around the right corner of house and can be heard entering the door.

Curtain.

Scene Two

The colour fades from the sky. Twilight begins. The interior of the kitchen is now visible. A pine table is at centre, a cooking-stove in the right rear corner, four rough wooden chairs, a tallow candle on the table. In the middle of the rear wall is fastened a big advertising poster with a ship in full sail and the word 'California' in big letters. Kitchen utensils hang from nails. Everything is neat and in order, but the atmosphere is of a men's camp kitchen rather than that of a home.

Places for three are laid. EBEN takes boiled potatoes and bacon from the stove and puts them on the table, also a loaf of bread and a crock of water. SIMEON and PETER shoulder in, slump down in their chairs without a word. EBEN joins them. The three eat in silence for a moment, the two elder as naturally unrestrained as beasts of the field, EBEN picking at his food without appetite, glancing at them with a tolerant dislike.

SIMEON (*suddenly turns to* EBEN.) Looky here! Ye'd oughtn't t' said that, Eben.

PETER. 'Twa'n't righteous.

EBEN. What?

SIMEON. Ye prayed he'd die.

EBEN. Waal – don't yew pray it? (*A pause.*)

PETER. He's our Paw.

EBEN (*violently*). Not mine!

SIMEON (*dryly*). Ye'd not let no one else say that about yer Maw! Ha! (*He gives one abrupt sardonic guffaw.* PETER *grins.*)

EBEN (*very pale*). I meant – I hain't his'n – I hain't like him – he hain't me –

PETER (*dryly*). Wait till ye've growed his age!

EBEN (*intensely*). I'm Maw – every drop of blood! (*A pause. They stare at him with indifferent curiosity.*)

PETER (*reminiscently*). She was good t'Sim 'n' me. A Good step-maw's scurse.

SIMEON. She was good t' every one.

EBEN (*greatly moved, gets to his feet and makes an awkward bow to each of them – stammering*). I be thankful t'ye. I'm her. Her heir. (*He sits down in confusion.*)

PETER (*after a pause— judicially*). She was good even t' him.

EBEN (*fiercely*). An' fur thanks he killed her!

SIMEON (*after a pause*). No one never kills nobody. It's allus somethin'. That's the murderer.

EBEN. Didn't he slave Maw t' death?

PETER. He's slaved himself t' death. He's slaved Sim 'n' me 'n' yew t' death – on'y none o' us hain't died – yit.

SIMEON. It's somethin' – drivin' him – t' drive us –

EBEN (*vengefully*). Waal – I hold him t' jedgement! (*Then scornfully.*) Somethin' ! What's somethin'?

SIMEON. Dunno.

EBEN (*sardonically*). What's drivin' yew to Californi-a, mebbe? (*They look at him in surprise.*) Oh, I've heerd ye! (*Then, after a pause.*) But ye'll never go t' the gold-fields!

PETER (*assertively*). Mebbe!

EBEN. Whar'll ye git the money?

PETER. We kin walk. It's an a'mighty ways – Californi-a – but if yew was t' put all the steps we've walked on this farm end t' end we'd be in the moon!

EBEN. The Injuns'll skulp ye on the plains.

SIMEON (*with grim humour*). We'll mebbe make 'em pay a hair fur a hair!

EBEN (*decisively*). But 'tain't that. Ye won't never go because ye'll wait here fur yer share o' the farm, thinkin' allus he'll die soon.

SIMEON (*after a pause*). We've a right.

PETER. Two-thirds belongs t' us.

EBEN (*jumping to his feet*). Ye've no right! She wa'n't yewr Maw! It was her farm! Didn't he steal it from her? She's dead. It's my farm.

SIMEON (*sardonically*). Tell that t' Paw – when he comes! I'll bet ye a dollar he'll laugh – fur once in his life. Ha! (*He laughs himself in one single mirthless bark.*)

PETER (*amused in turn, echoes his brother*). Ha!

SIMEON (*after a pause*). What've ye got held agin us, Eben? Year arter year it's skulked in yer eye – somethin'.

PETER. Ay-eh.

EBEN. Ay-eh. They's somethin'. (*Suddenly exploding.*) Why didn't ye never stand between him 'n' my Maw when he was slavin' her to her grave – t' pay her back fur the kindness she done t' yew? (*There is a long pause. They stare at him in surprise.*)

SIMEON. Waal – the stock'd got t' be watered.

PETER. 'R they was woodin' t' do.

SIMEON. 'R ploughin'.

PETER. 'R hayin'.

SIMEON. 'R spreadin' manure.

PETER. 'R weedin'.

SIMEON. 'R prunin'.

PETER. 'R milkin'.

EBEN (*breaking in harshly*). An' makin' walls – stone atop o' stone – makin' walls till yer heart's a stone ye heft up out o' the way o' growth on to a stone wall t' wall in yer heart!

SIMEON (*matter of factly*). We never had no time t' meddle.

PETER (*to* EBEN). Yew was fifteen afore yer Maw died – an' big fur yer age. Why didn't ye never do nothin'?

EBEN (*harshly*). They was chores t' do, wa'n't they? (*A pause – then slowly.*) It was on'y arter she died I come to think o' it. Me cookin' – doin' her work – that made me know her, suffer her sufferin' she'd come back t' help – come back t' bile potatoes – come back t' fry bacon – come back t' bake biscuits — come back all cramped up t' shake the fire, an' carry ashes, her eyes weepin' an' bloody with smoke an' cinders same's they used t' be. She still comes back – stands by the stove thar in the evenin' – she can't find it natoral sleepin' an' restin' in peace. She can't git used t' bein free – even in her grave.

SIMEON. She never complained none.

EBEN. She'd got too tired. She'd got too used t' bein too tired. That was what he done. (*With vengeful passion.*) An sooner'r later, I'll meddle. I'll say the thin's I didn't say then t' him! I'll yell 'em at the top o' my lungs. I'll see t' it my Maw gits some rest an' sleep in her grave! (*He sits down again, relapsing into a brooding silence. They look at him with a queer indifferent curiosity.*)

PETER (*after a pause*). Whar in tarnation d'ye s'pose he went, Sim?

SIMEON. Dunno. He druv off in the buggy, all spick an' span, with the mare all breshed an' shiny, druv off clackin' his tongue an' wavin' his whip. I remember it right well. I was finishin' ploughin', it was spring an' May an' sunset, an' gold in the West, an' he druv off into it. I yells 'Whar ye goin', Paw?' an' he hauls up by the stone wall a jiffy. His old snake's eyes was glitterin' in the sun like he'd been drinkin' a jugful an' he says with a mule's grin: 'Don't ye run away till I come back!'

PETER. Wonder if he knowed we was wantin' fur Californi-a?

SIMEON. Mebbe. I didn't say nothin' and he says, lookin' kinder queer an' sick: 'I been hearin' the hens cluckin' an' the roosters crowin' all the durn day. I been listenin' t' the cows lowin' an' everythin' else kickin' up till I can't stand it no more. It's spring an' I'm feelin' damned,' he says. 'Damned like an old bare hickory tree fit on'y fur burnin',' he says. An' then I calc'late I must've looked a mite hopeful, fur he adds real spry and vicious: 'But don't git no fool idee I'm dead. I've sworn t' live a hundred an' I'll do it, if on'y t' spite yer sinful greed! An' now I'm ridin' out t' learn God's message t' me in the spring, like the prophets done. An' yew git back t' yer ploughin',' he says. An' he druv off singin' a hymn. I thought he was drunk – 'r I'd stopped him goin'.

EBEN (*scornfully*). No, ye wouldn't! Ye're scared o' him. He's stronger – inside – than both o' ye put together!

PETER (*sardonically*). An' yew – be yew Samson?

EBEN. I'm gittin' stronger. I kin feel it growin' in me – growin' an' growin' – till it'll bust out – ! (*He gets up and puts on his coat and a hat. They watch him, gradually breaking into grins. EBEN avoids their eyes sheepishly.*) I'm goin' out fur a spell - up the road.

PETER. T' the village?

SIMEON. T' see Minnie?

EBEN (*defiantly*). Ay-eh!

PETER (*jeeringly*). The Scarlet Woman!

SIMEON. Lust – that's what's growin' in ye!

EBEN. Waal – she's purty!

PETER. She's been purty fur twenty year!

SIMEON. A new coat o' paint'll make a heifer out of forty.

EBEN. She hain't forty!

PETER. If she hain't, she's teeterin' on the edge.

EBEN (*desperately*). What d'yew know – ?

PETER. All they is . . . Sim knew her – an' then me arter –

SIMEON. An' Paw kin tell yew somethin', too! He was fust!

EBEN. D'ye mean t' say he –?

SIMEON (*with a grin*). Ay-eh! We air his heirs in everythin'!

EBEN (*intensely*). That's more to it! That grows on it! It'll bust soon! (*Then violently.*) I'll go smash my fist in her face! (*He pulls open the rear door violently.*)

SIMEON (*with a wink at* PETER— *drawlingly*). Mebbe – but the night's wa'm purty – by the time ye git thar mebbe ye'll kiss her instead!

PETER. Sart'n he will!

They both roar with coarse laughter. EBEN rushes out and slams the door – then the outside front door - comes around the corner of the house and stands still by the gate, staring up at the sky.

SIMEON (*looking after him*). Like his Paw!

PETER. Dead spit an' image!

SIMEON. Dog'll eat dog!

PETER. Ay-eh. (*Pause. With yearning.*) Mebbe a year from now we'll be in Californi-a.

SIMEON. Ay-eh. (*A pause. Both yawn.*) Let's git t' bed.

He blows out the candle. They go out door in rear. EBEN *stretches his arms up to the sky — rebelliously.*

EBEN. Waal - thar's a star, an' somewhar's they's him, an' here's me, an' thar's Min up the road - in the same night. What if I does kiss her? She's like t'night, she's soft 'n' wa'm, her eyes kin wink like a star, her mouth's wa'm, her arms're wa'm, she smells like a wa'm ploughed field, she's purty . . . Ay-eh! By God A'mighty she's purty, an' I don't give a damn how many sins she's sinned afore mine or who she's sinned 'em with, my sin's as purty as any one on 'em! (*He strides off down the road to the left.*)

Scene Three

It is the pitch darkness just before dawn. EBEN *comes in from the left and goes around to the porch, feeling his way, chuckling bitterly and cursing half-aloud to himself.*

EBEN. The cussed old miser! (*He can be heard going in the front door. There is a pause as he goes upstairs, then a loud knock on the bedroom door of the brothers.*) Wake up!

SIMEON (*startled*). Who's thar?

EBEN (*pushing open the door and coming in, a lighted candle in his hand. The bedroom of the brothers is revealed. Its ceiling is the sloping roof. They can stand upright only close to the centre dividing wall of the upstairs.* SIMEON *and* PETER *are in a double bed, front.* EBEN's *cot is to the rear.* EBEN *has a mixture of silly grin and vicious scowl on his face.*) I be!

PETER (*angrily*). What in hell fire –

EBEN. I got news fur ye! Ha! (*He gives one abrupt sardonic guffaw.*)

SIMEON (*angrily*). Couldn't ye hold it 'till we'd got our sleep?

EBEN. It's nigh sun up. (*Then explosively.*) He's gone an' married agen!

SIMEON *and* PETER (*explosively*). Paw?

EBEN. Got himself hitched to a female 'bout thirty-five – an purty, they says –

SIMEON (*aghast*). It's a durn lie!

PETER. Who says?

SIMEON. They been stringin' ye!

EBEN. Think I'm a dunce, do ye? The hull village says. The preacher from New Dover, he brung the news – told it t' our preacher - New Dover, that's whar the old loon got himself hitched – that's whar the woman lived –

PETER (*no longer doubting – stunned*). Waal . . .!

SIMEON (*the same*). Waal . . .!

EBEN (*sitting down on a bed – with vicious hatred*). Ain't he a devil out o' hell? It's jest t' spite us – the damned old mule!

PETER (*after a pause*). Everythin'll go t' her now.

SIMEON. Ay-eh. (*A pause – dully*). Waal – if it's done –

PETER. It's done us. (*Pause – then persuasively.*) They's gold in the fields o' Californi-a, Sim. No good a-stayin' here now.

SIMEON. Jest what I was a-thinkin'. (*Then with decision.*) 'S well fust's last! Let's lightout and git this mornin'.

PETER. Suits me.

EBEN. Ye must like walkin'

SIMEON (*sardonically*). If ye'd grow wings on us we'd fly thar!

EBEN. Ye'd like ridin' better – on a boat, wouldn't ye? (*Fumbles in his pocket and takes out a crumpled sheet of foolscap.*) Waal, if ye sign this ye kin ride on a boat. I've had it writ out an' ready in case ye'd ever go. It says fur three hundred dollars t' each ye agree yewr shares o' the farm is sold t' me. (*They look suspiciously at the paper. A pause.*)

SIMEON (*wonderingly*). But if he's hitched agen –

PETER. An' whar'd yew git that sum o' money, anyways?

EBEN (*cunningly*). I know whar it's hid. I been waitin' - Maw told me. She knew whar it lay fur years, but she was waitin' . . . It's her'n – the money he hoarded from her farm an' hid from Maw. It's my money by rights now.

PETER. Whar's it hid?

EBEN (*cunningly*). Whar yew won't never find it without me. Maw spied on him – 'r she'd never knowed. (*A pause. They look at him suspiciously, and he at them.*) Waal, is it fa'r trade?

SIMEON. Dunno.

PETER. Dunno.

SIMEON (*looking at window*). Sky's greyin'.

PETER. Ye better start the fire, Eben.

SIMEON. An fix some vittles.

EBEN. Ay-eh. (*Then with a forced jocular heartiness.*) I'll git ye a good one. If ye're startin' t' hoof it t' California ye'll need somethin' that'll stick t' yer ribs. (*He turns to the door, adding meaningly.*) But ye kin ride on a boat if ye'll swap. (*He stops at the door and pauses. They stare at him.*)

SIMEON (*suspiciously*). Whar was ye all night?

EBEN (*defiantly*). Up t' Min's (*Then slowly.*) Walkin' thar, fust I felt 's if I'd kiss her; then I got a-thinkin' o' what ye'd said o' him an' her an' I says, I'll but her nose fur that! Then I got t' the village an' heerd the news an' I got madder'n hell an' run all the way t' Min's not knowin' what I'd do – (*He pauses – then sheepishly but more defiantly.*) Waal – when I seen her, I didn't hit her – nor I didn't kiss her nuther – I begun t' beller like a calf an' cuss at the same time, I was so durn mad – an' she got scared – an' I jest grabbed holt an' tuk her! (*Proudly.*) Yes, sirree! I tuk her. She may've been his'n – an' your'n too - but she's mine now!

SIMEON (*dryly*). In love, air yew?

EBEN (*with lofty scorn*). Love! I don't take no stock in sech slop!

PETER (*winking at SIMEON*). Mebbe Eben's aimin' t' marry, too.

SIMEON. Min'd make a true faithful he'pmeet – fur the army! (*They snicker.*)

EBEN. What do I care fur her – 'ceptin' she's round an' wa'm? The p'int is she was his'n – an' now she b'longs t' me! (*He goes to the door— then turns – rebelliously.*) An' Min hain't sech a bad un. They's worse'n Min in the world, I'll bet ye! Wait'll we see this cow the Old man's hitched t'! She'll beat Min, I got a notion! (*He starts to go out.*)

SIMEON (*suddenly*). Mebbe ye'll try t' make her your'n, too?

PETER. Ha! (*He gives a sardonic laugh of relish at this idea.*)

EBEN (*spitting wth disgust*). Her – here – sleepin' with him - stealin' my Maw's farm! I'd as soon pet a skunk 'r kiss a snake! (*He goes out. The two stare after him suspiciously. A pause. They listen to his steps receding.*)

PETER. He's startin' the fire.

SIMEON. I'd like t' ride t' Californi-a – but –

PETER. Min might 'a' put some scheme in his head.

SIMEON. Mebbe it's all a lie 'bout Paw marryin'. We'd best wait an' see the bride.

PETER. An' don't sign nothin' till we does –

SIMEON. Nor till we've tested it's good money! (*Then with a grin.*) But if Paw's hitched we'd be sellin' Eben somethin' we'd never git nohow!

PETER. We'll wait an' see. (*Then with sudden vindictive anger.*) An' till he comes, let's yew 'n' me not wuk a lick, let Eben tend to thin's if he's a mind t', let's us jest sleep an' eat an' drink likker, an' let the hull damned farm go t' blazes!

SIMEON (*excitedly*). By God, we've 'arned a rest! We'll play rich fur a change. I hain't a-goin' to stir outa bed till breakfast's ready.

PETER. An' on the table!

SIMEON (*after a pause — thoughtfully*). What d'ye calc'late she'll be like – our new Maw? Like Eben thinks?

PETER. More'n likely.

SIMEON (*vindictively*). Waal – I hope she's a she-devil that'll make him wish he was dead an' livin' in the pit o' hell fur comfort!

PETER (*fervently*). Amen!

SIMEON (*imitating his father's voice*). 'I'm ridin' out t' learn God's message t' me in the spring like the prophets done,' he says. I'll bet right then an' thar he knew plumb well he was goin' whorin', the stinkin' old hypocrite!

Scene Four

Same as Scene Two – shows the interior of the kitchen, with a lighted candle on table. It is grey dawn outside. SIMEON *and* PETER *are just finishing their breakfast.* EBEN *sits before his plate of untouched food, brooding frowningly.*

PETER (*glancing at him rather irritably*). Lookin' glum don't help none.

SIMEON. (*sarcastically*). Sorrowin' over his lust o' the flesh.

PETER (*with a grin*). Was she yer fust?

EBEN (*angrily*). None o' yer business. (*A pause.*) I was thinkin' o' him. I got a notion he's gittin' near – I kin feel him comin' on like yew kin feel malaria chill afore it takes ye.

PETER. It's too early yet.

SIMEON. Dunno. He'd like t' catch us nappin – jest t' have somethin' t' hoss us 'round over.

PETER (*mechanically gets to his feet. SIMEON does the same*). Waal – let's git t' wuk. (*They both plod mechanically toward the door before they realise. Then they stop short.*)

SIMEON (*grinning*). Ye're a cussed fool, Pete – and I be wuss! Let him see we hain't wukin'! We don't give a durn!

PETER (*as they go back to the table*). Not a damned durn! It'll serve t' show him we're done with him. (*They sit down again. EBEN stares from one to the other with surprise.*)

SIMEON (*grins at him*). We're aimin' t' start bein' lilies o' the field.

PETER. Nary a toil 'r spin 'r lick o' wuk do we put in!

SIMEON. Ye're sole owner - till he comes – that's what ye wanted. Waal, ye got t' be sole hand, too.

PETER. The cows air bellerin'. Ye better hustle at the milkin'.

EBEN (*with excited joy*). Ye mean ye'll sign the paper?

SIMEON (*dryly*). Mebbe.

PETER. Mebbe.

SIMEON. We're considerin'. (*Peremptorily.*) Ye better git t' wuk.

EBEN (*with queer excitement*). It's Maw's farm agen! It's my farm! Them's my cows! I'll milk my durn fingers off fur cows o' mine! (*He goes out door in rear, they stare after him indifferently.*)

SIMEON. Like his Paw.

PETER. Dead spit 'n' image!

SIMEON. Waal – let dog eat dog!

EBEN *comes out of front door and around the corner of the house. The sky is beginning to grow flushed with sunrise. EBEN stops by the gate and stares around him with glowing, possessive eyes. He takes in the whole farm with his embracing glance of desire.*

EBEN. It's purty! It's damned purty! It's mine! (*He suddenly throws his head back boldly and glares with hard, defiant eyes at the sky.*) Mine, d'y hear? Mine! (*He turns and walks quickly of left, rear, toward the barn. The two brothers light their pipes.*)

SIMEON (*putting his muddy boots up on the table, tilting back his chair, and puffing defiantly)*. Waal – this air solid comfort – fur once.

PETER. Ay-eh. (*He follows suit. A pause. Unconsciously they both sigh.*)

SIMEON (*suddenly*). He never was much o' a hand at milkin', Eben wa'n't.

PETER (*with a snort*). His hands air like hoofs! (*A pause.*)

SIMEON. Reach down the jug thar! Let's take a swaller. I'm feelin' kind o' low.

PETER. Good idee! (*He does so – gets two glasses – they pour out drinks of whisky.*) Here's t' gold in Californi-a!

SIMEON. An' luck t' find it! (*They drink — puff resolutely – sigh – take their feet down from the table.*)

PETER. Likker don't 'pear t' sot right.

SIMEON. We hain't used t' it this early. (*A pause. They become very restless.*)

PETER. Gittin' close in this kitchen.

SIMEON (*with immense relief*). Let's git a breath o' air.

They arise briskly and go out rear – appear around house and stop by the gate. They stare up at the sky with a numbed appreciation.

PETER. Purty!

SIMEON. Ay-eh. Gold's t' the East now.

PETER. Sun's startin' with us fur the Golden West.

SIMEON (*staring around the farm, his compressed lips tightened, unable to conceal his emotion*). Waal – it's our last mornin' – mebbe.

PETER (*the same*). Ay-eh.

SIMEON (*stamps his foot on the earth and addresses it desperately*). Waal – ye've thirty year o' me buried in ye – spread out over ye – blood an' bone an' sweat – rotted away – fertilizin' ye – richin' yer soul – prime manure, by God, that's what I been t' ye!

PETER. Ay-eh! An' me!

SIMEON. An' yew, Peter. (*He sighs – then spits.*) Waal – no use'n cryin' over spilt milk.

PETER. They's gold in the West – an' freedom mebbe. We been slaves t' stone walls here.

SIMEON (*defiantly*). We hain't nobody's slaves from this out – nor no thin's slaves nuther. (*A pause - restlessly.*) Speakin' o' milk, wonder how Eben's managin'?

PETER. I s'pose he's managin'.

SIMEON. Mebbe we'd ought t' help – this once.

PETER. Mebbe. The cows knows us.

SIMEON. An' likes us. They don't know him much.

PETER. An' the hosses, an' pigs, an' chickens. They don't know
him much.

SIMEON. They knows us like brothers – an' likes us! (*Proudly.*)
Hain't we raised 'em t' be fust-rate, number one prize stock?

PETER. We hain't – not no more.

SIMEON (*dully*). I was fergettin'. (*Then resignedly.*) Waal, let's go
help Eben a spell an' git waked up.

PETER. Suits me.

They are starting off down left, rear, for the barn when EBEN *appears
from there hurrying toward them, his face excited.*

EBEN (*breathlessly*). Waal - har they be! The old mule an' the bride!
I seen 'em from the barn down below at the turnin'.

PETER. How could ye tell that far?

EBEN. Hain't I as far-sight as he's near-sight? Don't I know the
mare 'n' buggy, an' two people settin' in it? Who else. . .? An' I
tell ye I kin feel 'em a-comin', too! (*He squirms as if he had the
itch.*)

PETER (*beginning to be angry*). Waal – let him do his own
unhitchin'!

SIMEON (*angry in his turn*). Let's hustle in an' git our bundles an'
be a-goin' as he's a-comin'. I don't want never t' step inside the
door agen arter he's back.

They both start back around the corner of the house. EBEN *follows
them.*

EBEN (*excitedly*). Will ye sign it afore ye go?

PETER. Let's see the colour o' the old skin-flint's money an' we'll
sign.

*They disappear left. The two brothers clump upstairs to get their
bundles.* EBEN *appears in the kitchen, runs to window, peers out,
comes back and pulls up a strip of flooring under stove, takes out a
canvas bag and puts it on table, then sets the floor-board back in place.
The two brothers appear a moment after. They carry old carpet bags.*)

EBEN (*puts his hand on bag guardingly*). Have ye signed?

SIMEON (*shows paper in his hand*). Ay-eh. (*Greedily.*) Be that the money?

EBEN (*opens bag and pours out pile of twenty-dollar gold pieces*). Twenty-dollar pieces – thirty on 'em. Count 'em. (PETER *does so, arranging them in stacks of five, biting one or two to test them.*)

PETER. Six hundred. (*He puts them in bag and puts it inside his shirt carefully.*)

SIMEON (*handing paper to* EBEN). Har ye be.

EBEN (*after a glance, folds it carefully and hides it under his shirt – gratefully*). Thank yew.

PETER. Thank yew fur the ride.

SIMEON. We'll send ye a lump o' gold fur Christmas. (*A pause. He stares at them and they at him.*)

PETER (*awkwardly*). Waal – we're a-goin'.

SIMEON. Comin' out t' the yard?

EBEN. No. I'm waitin' in here a spell. (*Another silence. The brothers edge awkwardly to door in rear– then turn and stand.*)

SIMEON. Waal – goodbye.

PETER. Goodbye.

EBEN. Goodbye.

> *They go out. He sits down at the table, faces the stove and pulls out the paper. He looks from it to the stove. His face, lighted up by the shaft of sunlight from the window, has an expression of trance. His lips move. The two brothers come out to the gate.*

PETER (*looking off toward barn*). Thar he be – unhitchin'.

SIMEON (*with a chuckle*). I'll bet ye he's riled!

PETER. An' thar she be.

SIMEON. Let's wait 'n' see what our new Maw looks like.

PETER (*with a grin*). An' give him our partin' cuss!

SIMEON (*grinning*). I feel like raisin' fun. I feel light in my head an' feet.

PETER. Me, too. I feel like laffin' till I'd split up the middle.

SIMEON. Reckon it's the likker?

PETER. No. My feet feel itchin' t' walk an' walk – an' jump high over thin's – an' –

SIMEON. Dance? (*A pause.*)

PETER (*puzzled*). It's plumb onnateral.

SIMEON (*a light coming over his face*). I calc'late it's 'cause school's out. It's holiday. Fur once we're free!

PETER (*dazedly*). Free?

SIMEON. The halter's broke – the harness is busted – the fence bars is down – the stone walls air crumblin' an' tumblin'! We'll be kickin' up an' tearin' away down the road!

PETER (*drawing a deep breath – oratorically*). Anybody that wants this stinkin' old-rock pile of a farm kin hev it. 'Tain't our'n, no sirree!

SIMEON (*takes the gate off its hinges and puts it under his arm*). We harby 'bolishes shet gates, an' open gates, an' all gates, by thunder!

PETER. We'll take it with us fur luck an' let 'er sail free down some river.

SIMEON (*as a sound of voices comes from left, rear*). Har they comes!

> *The two brothers congeal into two stiff, grim-visaged statues.*
> EPHRAIM CABOT *and* ABBIE PUTNAM *come in.* CABOT *is seventy-five, tall and gaunt, with great, wiry, concentrated power, but stoop-shouldered from toil. His face is as hard as if it were hewn out of a boulder, yet there is a weakness in it, a petty pride in its own narrow strength. His eyes are small, close together, and extremely near-sighted, blinking continually in the effort to focus on objects, their stare having a straining, ingrowing quality. He is dressed in his dismal black Sunday suit.* ABBIE *is thirty-five, buxom, full of vitality. Her round face is pretty, but marred by its rather gross sensuality. There is strength and obstinacy in her jaw, a hard determination in her eyes, and about her whole personality the same unsettled, untamed, desperate quality which is so apparent in* EBEN.

CABOT (*as they enter – a queer strangled emotion in his dry cracking voice*). Har we be t' hum, Abbie.

ABBIE (*with lust for the word*). Hum! (*Her eyes gloating on the house without seeming to see the two stiff figures at the gate.*) It's purty – purty! I can't b'lieve it's r'ally mine.

CABOT (*sharply*). Yewr'n? Mine! (*He stares at her penetratingly. She stares back. He adds relentingly.*) Our'n – mebbe! It was lonesome too long. I was growin' old in the spring. A hum's got t' hev a woman.

ABBIE (*her voice taking possession*). A woman's got t' hev a hum!

CABOT (*nodding uncertainly*). Ay-eh. (*Then irritably.*) Whar be they? Ain't thar nobody about –'r wukin' – 'r nothin'?

ABBIE (*sees the brothers. She returns their stare of cold appraising contempt with interest – slowly*). Thar's two men loafin' at the gate an' starin' at me like a couple o' strayed hogs.

CABOT (*straining his eyes*). I kin see 'em – but I can't make out –

SIMEON. It's Simeon.

PETER. It's Peter.

CABOT (*exploding*). Why hain't ye wukin'?

SIMEON (*dryly*). We're waitin' t' welcome ye hum – yew an' the bride!

CABOT (*confusedly*). Hunh? Waal – this be yer new Maw, boys. (*She stares at them and they at her.*)

SIMEON (*turns away and spits contemptuously*). I see her!

PETER (*spits also*). An' I see her!

ABBIE (*with the conqueror's conscious superiority*). I'll go in an' look at *my* house. (*She goes slowly around to porch.*)

SIMEON (*with a snort*). *Her* house!

PETER (*calls after her*). Ye'll find Eben inside. Ye better not tell him it's *yewr* house.

ABBIE (*mouthing the name*). Eben. (*Then quietly.*) I'll tell Eben.

CABOT (*with a contemptuous sneer*). Ye needn't heed Eben. Eben's a dumb fool – like his Maw – soft an' simple!

SIMEON (*with his sardonic burst of laughter*). Ha! Eben's a chip o' yew – spit 'n' image – hard 'n' bitter's a hickory tree! Dog'll eat dog. He'll eat ye yet, old man!

CABOT (*commandingly*). Ye git t' wuk!

SIMEON (*as ABBIE disappears in house – winks at PETER and says tauntingly*). So that thar's our new Maw, be it? Whar in hell did ye dig her up? (*He and PETER laugh.*)

PETER. Ha! Ye'd better turn her in the pen with the other sows. (*They laugh uproariously, slapping their thighs.*)

CABOT (*so amazed at their effrontery that he stutters in confusion*). Simeon! Peter! What's come over ye? Air ye drunk?

SIMEON. We're free, old man – free o' yew an' the hull damned farm! (*They grow more and more hilarious and excited.*)

PETER. An' we're startin' out fur the gold-fields o' Californi-a!

SIMEON. Ye kin take this place an' burn it!

PETER. An' bury it – fur all we cares!

SIMEON. We're free, old man! (*He cuts a caper.*)

PETER. Free. (*He gives a kick in the air.*)

SIMEON (*in a frenzy*). Whoop!

PETER. Whoop! (*They do an absurd Indian war dance about the old man, who is petrified between rage and the fear that they are insane.*)

SIMEON. We're free as Injuns! Lucky we don't skulp ye!

PETER. An' burn yer barn an' kill the stock!

SIMEON. An' rape yer new woman! Whoop! (*He and* PETER *stop their dance, holding their sides, rocking with wild laughter.*)

CABOT (*edging away*). Lust fur gold – fur the sinful, easy gold o' Californi-a! It's made ye mad!

SIMEON (*tauntingly*). Wouldn't ye like us to send ye back some sinful gold, ye old sinner?

PETER. They's gold besides what's in Californi-a! (*He retreats back beyond the vision of the old man and takes the bag of money and flaunts it in the air above his head, laughing.*)

SIMEON. And sinfuller, too!

PETER. We'll be voyagin' on the sea! Whoop! (*He leaps up and down.*)

SIMEON. Livin' free! Whoop! (*He leaps in turn.*)

CABOT (*suddenly roaring with rage*). My cuss on ye!

SIMEON. Take our'n in trade fur it! Whoop!

CABOT. I'll hev ye both chained up in the asylum!

PETER. Ye old skinflint! Goodbye!

SIMEON. Ye old blood-sucker! Goodbye!

CABOT. Go afore I – !

PETER. Whoop! (*He picks a stone from the road.* SIMEON *does the same.*)

SIMEON. Maw'll be in the parlour.

PETER. Ay-eh! One! Two!

CABOT (*frightened*). What air ye - ?

PETER. Three! (*They both throw the stones hitting the parlour window with a crash of glass, tearing the shade.*)

SIMEON. Whoop!

PETER. Whoop!

CABOT (*in a fury now, rushing toward them*). If I kin lay hand on ye – I'll break yer bones fur ye!

But they beat a capering retreat before him, SIMEON with the gate still under his arm. CABOT comes back, panting wih impotent rage. Their voices as they go off take up the song of the gold-seekers to the old tune of "Oh, Susannah!"

'I jumped aboard the Liza ship,
And travelled on the sea,
And every time I thought of home
I wished it wasn't me!
Oh! Californi-a,
That's the land fur me!
I'm off to Californi-a!
With my wash-bowl on my knee.'

In the meantime the window of the upper bedroom on right is raised and ABBIE sticks her head out. She looks down at CABOT - with a sigh of relief.

ABBIE. Waal – that's the last o' them two, hain't it? (*He doesn't answer. Then in possessive tones.*) This here's a nice bedroom, Ephraim. It's a r'al nice bed.Is it my room, Ephraim?

CABOT (*grimly – without looking up*). Our'n! (*She cannot control a grimace of aversion and pulls back her head slowly and shuts the window. A sudden horrible thought seems to enter CABOT's head.*) They been up to somethin'! Mebbe – mebbe they've pizened the stock – 'r somethin'!

He almost runs off down toward the barn. A moment later the kitchen door is slowly pushed open and ABBIE enters. For a moment she stands looking at EBEN. He does not notice her at first. Her eyes take him in penetratingly with a calculating appraisal of his strength as against hers. But under this her desire is dimly awakened by his youth and good looks. Suddenly he becomes conscious of her presence and looks up. Their eyes meet: He leaps to his feet, glowering at her speechlessly.

ABBIE (*in her most seductive tones which she uses all through this scene*). Be you – Eben? I'm Abbie – (*She laughs.*) I mean, I'm yer new Maw.

EBEN (*viciously*). No, damn ye!

ABBIE (*as if she hadn't heard – with a queer smile*). Yer Paw's spoke a lot o' yew –

EBEN. Ha!

ABBIE. Ye mustn't mind him. He's an old man. (*A long pause. They stare at each other.*) I don't want t' pretend playin' Maw t' ye, Eben. (*Admiringly.*) Ye're too big an' too strong fur that. I want t' be fren's with ye. Mebbe with me fur a fren' ye'd find ye'd like livin' here better. I kin make it easy fur ye with him, mebbe. (*With a scornful sense of power.*) I calc'late I kin git him t'do most anythin' fur me.

EBEN (*with bitter scorn*). Ha! (*They stare again*, EBEN *obscurely moved, physically atracted to her – in forced stilted tones.*) Yew kin go t' the devil!

ABBIE (*calmly*). If cussin' me does ye good, cuss all ye've a mind t'. I'm all prepared t' hae ye agin me – at fust. I don't blame ye nuther. I'd feel the same at any stranger comin' t' take my Maw's place. (*He shudders. She is watching him carefully.*) Yew must've cared a lot fur yewr Maw, didn't ye? My Maw died afore I'd growed. I don't remember her none. (*A pause.*) But yew won't hate me long, Eben. I'm not the wust in the world – an yew an' me've got a lot in common. I kin tell that by lookin' at ye. Waal – I've had a hard life, too – oceans o' trouble an' nuthin' but wuk fur reward. I was a' orphan early an' had t' wuk fur others in others' hums. Then I married, an' he turned out a drunken spreer an' so he had to wuk fur others an' me too agen in others' hums, an' the baby died, an' my husband got sick an' died too, an' I was glad, sayin' now I'm free fur once, on'y I diskivered right away all I was free fur was t' wuk agen in others' hums, doin others' wuk in others' hums till I'd most give up hope o' ever doin' my own wuk in my own hum, an' then your Paw come –

CABOT *appears, returning from the barn. He comes to the gate and looks down the road the brothers have gone. A faint strain of their retreating voices is heard; 'Oh, Californi-a! That's the place for me.' He stands glowering, his fist clenched, his face grim with rage.*

EBEN (*fighting against his growing attraction and sympathy – harshly*). An' bought yew – like a harlot! (*She is stung and flushes angrily. She has been sincerely moved by the recital of her troubles. He adds furiously.*) An' the price he's payin' ye – this farm – was my Maw's damn ye! – an' mine now!

ABBIE (*with a cool laugh of confidence*). Yewr'n? We'll see 'bout that! (*Then strongly.*) Waal – what if I did need a hum? What else'd I marry an old man like him fur?

EBEN (*maliciously*). I'll tel him ye said that!

ABBIE (*smiling*). I'll say ye're a lying– a-purpose – an' he'll drive ye off the place!

EBEN. Ye devil!

ABBIE (*defying him*). This be my farm – this be my hum - this be my kitchen –!

EBEN (*furiously, as if he were going to attack her*). Shut up, damn ye!

ABBIE (*walks up to him – a queer coarse expression of desire in her face and body – slowly*). An' upstairs – that be my bedroom – an' my bed! (*He stares into her eyes, terribly confused and torn. She adds softly.*) I hain't bad nor mean – 'ceptin' fur an enemy – but I got t' fight fur what's due me out o' life, if I ever 'spect t' git it. (*Then putting her hand on his arm – seductively.*) Let's yew 'n' me be fren's, Eben.

EBEN (*stupidly – as if hypnotised*). Ay-eh. (*Then furiously flinging off her arm.*) No, ye durned old witch! I hate ye! (*He rushes out the door.*)

ABBIE (*looks after him, smiling satisfiedly - then half to herself, mouthing the word*). Eben's nice. (*She looks at the table, proudly.*) I'll wash up my dishes now. (EBEN *appears outside, slamming the door behind him. He comes around corner, stops on seeing his father, and stands staring at him with hate.*)

CABOT (*raising his arms to Heaven in the fury he can no longer control*). Lord God o' Hosts, smite the undutiful sons with Thy wust cuss.

EBEN (*breaking in violently*). Yew 'n' yewr God! Allus cussin folks – allus naggin' em!

CABOT (*oblivious to him — summoningly*). God o' the old! God o' the lonesome!

EBEN (*mockingly*). Naggin' His sheep t' sin! T' hell with yewr God!

CABOT (*wrathfully*). 'The days air prolonged and every vision faileth!'

EBEN (*spitting*). Good enuf for ye! (CABOT *turns. He and* EBEN *glower at each other.*)

CABOT (*harshly*). So it's yew. I might've knowed it. (*Shaking his finger threateningly at him.*) Blasphemin' fool! (*Then quickly.*) Why hain't ye t' wuk?

EBEN. Why hain't yew? They've went. I can't wuk it all alone.

CABOT (*contemptuously*). Nor noways! I'm wuth ten o' ye yit, old's I be! Ye'll never be more'n half a man! (*Then, matter-of-factly.*) Waal – let's git t' the barn.

They go. A last faint note of the 'California' *song is heard from the distance.* ABBIE *is washing the dishes.*

Curtain.

PART TWO

Scene One

The exterior of the farm-house, as in Part One – a hot Sunday afternoon two months later. ABBIE dressed in her best, is discovered sitting in a rocker at the end of the porch. She rocks listlessly, enervated by the heat, staring in front of her with bored, half-closed eyes

EBEN *sticks his head out of his bedroom window. He looks around furtively and tries to see – or hear – if anyone is on the porch, but although he has been careful to make no noise, ABBIE has sensed his movement. She stops rocking, her face grows animated and eager, she waits attentively. EBEN seems to feel her presence, he scowls back his thoughts of her and spits with exaggerated disdain – then withdraws back into the room. ABBIE waits, holding her breath as she listens with passionate eagerness for every sound within the house.*

EBEN *comes out. Their eyes meet. His falter, he is confused, he turns away and slams the door resentfully. At this gesture, ABBIE laughs tantalisingly, amused, but at the same time piqued and irritated. He scowls, strides off the porch to the path and starts to walk past her to the road with a grand swagger of ignoring her existence. He is dressed in his store suit, spruced up, his face shines from soap and water.*

ABBIE *leans forward on her chair, her eyes hard and angry now, and, as he passes her, gives a sneering, taunting chuckle.*

EBEN (*stung – turns on her furiously*). What air yew cacklin, 'bout?

ABBIE (*triumphantly*). Yew!

EBEN. What about me?

ABBIE. Ye look all slicked up like a prize bull.

EBEN (*with a sneer*). Waal – ye hain't so durned purty yerself, be ye? (*They stare into each other's eyes, his held by hers in spite of himself, hers glowingly possessive. Their physical attraction becomes a palpable force quivering in the hot air.*)

ABBIE (*softly*). Ye don't mean that, Eben. Ye may think ye mean it, mebbe, but ye don't. Ye can't. It's agin nature, Eben. Ye been fightin' yer nature ever since the day I come – tryin' t' tell yerself I hain't purty t' ye. (*She laughs a low humid laugh without taking her eyes from his. A pause – her body squirms desirously – she murmurs languorously.*) Hain't the sun strong an' hot? Ye kin feel

it burnin' into the earth – Nature – makin' thin's grow – bigger
'n' bigger – burnin' inside ye – makin' ye want t' grow – into
somethin' else – till ye're jined with it 'an it's your'n – but it
owns ye, too – an' makes ye grow bigger – like a tree – like them
elums – (*She laughs again softly, holding his eyes. He takes a step
toward her, compelled against his will.*) Nature'll beat ye, Eben. Ye
might's well own up t' it fust's last.

EBEN (*trying to break from her spell – confusedly*). If Paw'd hear ye
goin' on . . . (*Resentfully.*) But ye've made such a damned idjit
out o' the old devil. . . (ABBIE *laughs.*)

ABBIE. Waal – hain't it easier fur yew with him changed softer?

EBEN (*defiantly*). No. I'm fightin' him – fightin yew – fightin fur
Maw's rights t' her hum! (*This breaks her spell for him. He glowers
at her.*) An' I'm on to ye. Ye hain't foolin' me a mite. Ye're
aimin' t' swaller up everythin' an' make it your'n. Waal, you'll
find I'm a heap sight bigger hunk nor yew kin chew! (*He turns
from her with a sneer.*)

ABBIE (*trying to regain her ascendancy – seductively*). Eben!

EBEN. Leave me be! (*He starts to walk away.*)

ABBIE (*more commandingly*). Eben!

EBEN (*stops – resentfully*). What d'ye want?

ABBIE (*trying to conceal a growing excitement*). Whar air ye goin'?

EBEN (*with malicious nonchalance*). Oh – up the road a spell.

ABBIE. T' the village?

EBEN (*airily*). Mebbe.

ABBIE (*excitedly*). T' see that Min, I s'pose?

EBEN. Mebbe.

ABBIE (*weakly*). What d'ye want t' waste time on her fur?

EBEN (*revenging himself now – grinning at her*). Ye can't beat Nature,
didn't ye say? (*He laughs and again starts to walk away.*)

ABBIE (*bursting out*). An ugly old hake!

EBEN (*with a tantalising sneer*). She's purtier'n yew be!

ABBIE. That every wuthless drunk in the country has. . .

EBEN (*tauntingly*). Mebbe – but she's better'n yew. She owns up
f'ar 'n' squ'ar t' her doin's.

ABBIE (*furiously*). Don't ye dare compare –

EBEN. She don't go sneakin' an' stealin' – what's mine.

ABBIE (*savagely seizing on his weak point*). Your'n? Yew mean – my farm!

EBEN. I mean the farm yew sold yerself fur like any other old whore – my farm!

ABBIE (*stung—fiercely*) Ye'll never live t' see the day when even a stinkin' weed on it'll belong t'ye! (*Then in a scream.*) Git out o' my sight! Go on t' yer slut – disgracin' yer Paw 'n' me! I'll git yer Paw t' horsewhip ye off the place if I want t'! Ye're only livin' here cause I tolerate ye! Git along! I hate the sight o' ye! (*She stops, panting and glaring at him.*)

EBEN (*returning her glance in kind*). An' I hate the sight o' yew!

He turns and strides off up the road. She follows his retreating figure with concentrated hate. Old CABOT *appears coming up from the barn. The hard, grim expression of his face has changed. He seems in some queer way softened, mellowed. His eyes have taken on a strange, incongruous dreamy quality. Yet there is no hint of physical weakness about him – rather he looks more robust and younger.* ABBIE *sees him and turns away quickly with unconcealed aversion. He comes slowly up to her.*

CABOT (*mildly*). War yew an' Eben quarrellin' agin?

ABBIE (*shortly*). No.

CABOT. Ye was talkin' a'mighty loud . . . (*He sits down on the edge of the porch.*)

ABBIE (*snappishly*). If ye heerd us they hain't no need askin' questions.

CABOT. I didn't hear what ye said.

ABBIE (*relieved*). Waal – it wa'n't nothin' t' speak on.

CABOT (*after a pause*). Eben's queer.

ABBIE (*bitterly*). He's the dead spit 'n' image o' yew!

CABOT (*queerly interested*). D'ye think so, Abbie? (*After a pause, ruminatingly.*) Me 'n' Eben's allus fit 'n' fit. I never could b'ar him noways. He's so thunderin' soft – like his Maw.

ABBIE (*scornfully*). Ay-eh! 'Bout as soft as yew be!

CABOT (*as if he hadn't heard*). Mebbe I been too hard on him.

ABBIE (*jeeringly*). Waal – ye're gittin' soft now – soft as slop! That's what Eben was sayin'.

CABOT (*his face instantly grim and ominous*). Eben was sayin? Waal, he'd best not do nothin' t' try me 'r he'll soon diskiver . . . (*A pause. She keeps her face turned away. His gradually softens. He stares up at the sky.*) Purty, hain't it?

ABBIE (*crossly*). I don't see nothin' purty.

CABOT. The sky. Feels like a warm field up thar.

ABBIE (*sarcastically*). Air yew aimin' t' buy up over the farm, too? (*She snickers contemptuously.*)

CABOT (*strangely*). I'd like t' own my place up thar. (*A pause.*) I'm getting old, Abbie. I'm gittin' ripe on the bough. (*A pause. She stares at him mystified. He goes on.*) It's allus lonesome cold in the house – even when it's bilin' hot outside. Hain't yew noticed?

ABBIE. No.

CABOT. It's warm down t' the barn – nice smellin' an' warm – with the cows. (*A pause.*) Cows is queer.

ABBIE. Like yew!

CABOT. Like Eben. (*A pause.*) I'm gittin' t' feel resigned t' Eben – jest as I got t' feel 'bout his Maw. I'm gittin' t' learn to b'ar his softness – jest like her'n. I cal'clate I c'd a'most take t' him – if he wa'n't sech a dumb fool! (*A pause.*) I s'pose it's old age a-creepin' in my bones.

ABBIE (*indifferently*). Waal – ye hain't dead yet.

CABOT (*roused*). No, I hain't, yew bet – not by a hell of a sight – I'm sound 'n' tough as hickory! (*Then moodily.*) But arter three score and ten the Lord warns ye t' prepare. (*A pause.*) That's why Eben's come in my head. Now that his cussed sinful brothers is gone their path t' hell, they's no one left but Eben.

ABBIE (*resentfully*). They's me, hain't they? (*Agitatedly.*) What's all this sudden likin' ye've tuk to Eben? Why don't ye say nothin' 'bout me? Hain't I yer lawful wife?

CABOT (*simply*). Ay-eh. Ye be. (*A pause he stares at her desirously – his eyes grow avid – then with a sudden movement he seizes her hands and squeezes them, declaiming in a queer camp-meeting preacher's tempo.*) Yew air my Rose o' Sharon! Behold, yew air fair; yer eyes air doves; yer lips air like scarlet; yer two breasts air like two fawns; yer navel be like a round goblet; yer belly be like a heap o' wheat. . . (*He covers her hand with kisses. She does not seem to notice. She stares before her with hard angry eyes.*)

ABBIE (*jerking her hands away – harshly*). So ye're plannin' t' leave the farm t' Eben, air ye?

CABOT (*dazedly*). Leave. . . ? (*Then with resentful obstinacy.*) I hain't a-givin' it t' no one!

ABBIE (*remorselessly*). Ye can't take it with ye.

CABOT (*thinks a moment – then reluctantly*). No, I calc'late not. (*After a pause – with a strange passion.*) But if I could, I would, by the Eternal! 'R if I could, in my dyin' hour, I'd set it afire an' watch it burn – this house an' every ear o' corn an' every tree down t' the last blade o' hay! I'd sit an' know it was all a-dying with me an' no one else'd ever own what was mine, what I'd made out o' nothin' with my own sweat 'n' blood! (*A pause – then he adds with a queer affection.*) 'Ceptin' the cows. Them I'd turn free.

ABBIE (*harshly*). An' me?

CABOT (*with a queer smile*). Ye'd be turned free, too.

ABBIE (*furiously*). So that's the thanks I git fur marryin' ye - t' have ye change kind to Eben who hates ye, an' talk o' turnin' me out in the road.

CABOT (*hastily*). Abbie! Ye know I wa'n't . . .

ABBIE (*vengefully*). Just let me tell ye a thing or two 'bout Eben! Whar's he's gone? T' see that harlot, Min! I tried fur t' stop him. Disgracin' yew an' me - on the Sabbath, too!

CABOT (*rather guiltily*). He's a sinner – nateral-born. It's lust eatin' his heart.

ABBIE (*enraged beyond endurance – wildly vindictive*). An' his lust fur me! Kin ye find excuses fur that?

CABOT (*stares at her – after a dead pause*). Lust – fur yew?

ABBIE (*defiantly*). He was tryin' t' make love t' me – when ye heerd us quarrellin'.

CABOT (*stares at her – then a terrible expression of rage comes over his face – he springs to his feet shaking all over*). By the A'mighty God – I'll end him!

ABBIE (*frightened now for* EBEN). No! Don't ye!

CABOT (*violently*). I'll git the shotgun an' blow his soft brains t' the top o' them elums!

ABBIE (*throwing her arms around him*). No, Ephraim!

CABOT (*pushing her away violently*). I will, by God!

ABBIE (*in a quieting tone*). Listen, Ephraim. T'wa'n't nothin' bad – on'y a boy's foolin' – t'wa'n't meant serious – jest jokin' an teasin' . . .

CABOT. Then why did ye say – lust?

ABBIE. It must hev sounded wusser'n I meant. An' I was mad at thinkin' – ye'd leave him the farm.

CABOT (*quieter, but still grim and cruel*). Waal then, I'll horsewhip him off the place if that much'll content ye.

ABBIE (*reaching out and taking his hand*). No. Don't think o' me! Ye mustn't drive him off. T'ain't sensible. Who'll ye get to help ye on the farm? They's no one hereabouts.

CABOT (*considers this – then nodding his appreciation*). Ye got a head on ye. (*Then irritably.*) Waal, let him stay. (*He sits down on the edge of the porch. She sits beside him. He murmurs contemptuously.*) I oughtn't t' git riled so – at that 'ere fool calf. (*A pause.*) But har's the p'int. What son o' mine'll keep on here t' the farm – when the Lord does call me? Simeon an' Peter air gone t' hell – an Eben's follerin' 'em –

ABBIE. They's me.

CABOT. Ye're on'y a woman.

ABBIE. I'm yewr wife.

CABOT. That hain't me. A son is me – my blood – mine. Mine ought t' git mine. An' then it's still mine – even though I be six foot under. D'ye see?

ABBIE (*giving him a look of hatred*). Ay-eh. I see. (*She becomes very thoughtful, her face growing shrewd, her eyes studying CABOT craftily.*)

CABOT. I'm gittin' old – ripe on the bough. (*Then with a sudden forced reassurance.*) Not but what I hain't a hard nut t' crack even yet – an' fur many a year t' come! By the Etarnal, I kin break most o' the young fellers' back at any kind o' work any day o' the year!

ABBIE (*suddenly*). Mebbe the Lord'll give *us* a son.

CABOT (*turns and stares at her eagerly*). Ye mean – a son – t' me 'n' yew?

ABBIE (*with a cajoling smile*). Ye're a strong man, yet, hain't ye? 'Tain't noways impossible, be it? We know that. Why d'ye stare so? Hain't ye never thought o' that afore? I been thinkin' o' it all along. Ay-eh 'an' I been prayin' it'd happen, too.

CABOT (*his face growing full of joyous pride and a sort of religious ecstasy*). Ye been prayin', Abbie? – fur a son? – t' us?

ABBIE. Ay-eh. (*With a grim resolution.*) I want a son now.

CABOT (*excitedly clutching both of her hands in his*). It'd be the blessin' o' God, Abbie – the blessin' o' God A'mighty on me – in my old age – in my lonesomeness! They hain't nothin' I wouldn't do fur ye then, Abbie. Ye'd hev on'y t' ask it – anythin' ye'd a mind t' –

ABBIE (*interrupting*). Would ye will the farm t' me then – t' me an' it?

CABOT (*vehemently*). I'd do anythin' ye axed, I tell ye! I swear it! May I be everlastin' damned t' hell if I wouldn't! (*He sinks to his knees, pulling her down with him. He trembles all over with the fervour of his hopes.*) Pray t' the Lord agin, Abbie. It's the Sabbath! I'll jine ye! Two prayers air better nor one. 'An' God hearkened unto Rachel an' she conceived an' bore a son.' An' God hearkened unto Abbie! Pray, Abbie! Pray fur Him to hearken! (*He bows his head, mumbling. She pretends to do likewise, but gives him a side glance of scorn and triumph.*)

Scene Two

About eight in the evening. The interior of the two bedrooms on the top floor is shown. EBEN is sitting on the side of his bed in the room on the left. On account of the heat he has taken off everything but his undershirt and pants. His feet are bare. He faces front, brooding moodily, his chin propped on his hands, a desperate expression on his face.

In the other room CABOT and ABBIE are sitting side by side on the edge of their bed, an old fourposter with feather mattress. He is in his night-shirt, she in her night-dress. He is still in the queer excited mood into whch the notion of a son has thrown him. Both rooms are lighted dimly and flickeringly by tallow candles.

CABOT. The farm needs a son.

ABBIE. I need a son.

CABOT. Ay-eh. Sometimes ye air the farm an' sometimes the farm be yew. That's why I clove t' ye in my lonesomeness. (*A pause. He pounds his knee with his fist.*) Me an' the farm has got t' beget a son!

ABBIE. Ye'd best go t' sleep. Ye're gittin' thin's all mixed.

CABOT. (*with an impatient gesture*). No, I hain't. My mind's clear's a well. Ye don't know me, that's it. (*He stares hopelessly at the floor.*)

ABBIE (*indifferently*). Mebbe.

In the next room EBEN gets up and paces up and down distractedly. ABBIE hears him. Her eyes fasten on the intervening wall with concentrated attention. EBEN stops and stares. Their hot glances seem to meet through the wall. Unconsciously he stretches out his arms for her and she half rises. Then aware, he mutters a curse at himself and flings himself face downward on the bed, his clenched fists above his head, his face buried in the pillow. ABBIE relaxes with a faint sigh, but her eyes remain fixed on the wall, she listens with all her attention for some movement from EBEN.

CABOT (*suddenly raises his head and looks at her – scornfully*). Will ye ever know me – 'r will any man 'r woman? (*Shaking his head.*) No. I calc'late 't wa'n't t' be. (*He turns away.* ABBIE *looks at the wall. Then, evidently unable to keep silent about his thoughts, without looking at his wife, he puts out his hand and clutches her knee. She starts violently, looks at him, sees he is not watching her, concentrates again on the wall and pays no attention to what he says.*) Listen, Abbie. When I come here fifty odd year ago – I was jest twenty an' the strongest an' hardest ye ever seen – ten times as strong an' fifty times as hard as Eben. Waal – this place was nothin' but fields o' stones. Folks laughed when I tuk it. They couldn't know what I knowed. When ye kin make corn sprout out o' stones, God's livin' in yew. They wa'n't strong enuf fur that! They reckoned God was easy. They laughed. They don't laugh no more. Some died hereabouts. Some went West an' died. They're all under ground – fur follerin' arter an easy God. God hain't easy. (*He shakes his head slowly.*) An' I growed hard. Folks kept allus sayin', 'He's a hard man,' like 'twas sinful t' be hard, so's at last I said back 'em, 'Waal then, by thunder, ye'll git me hard an' see how ye like it!' (*Then suddenly.*) But I give in t' weakness once. 'Twas arter I'd been here two year. I got weak – despairful – they was so many stones. They was a party leavin', givin' up, goin' West. I jined 'em. We tracked on 'n on. We come t' broad medders, plains, whar the soil was black an' rich as gold. Nary a stone. Easy. Ye'd on'y to plough an' sow an' then set an' smoke yer pipe an' watch thin's grow. I could o' been a rich man – but somethin' in me fit me an' fit me – the voice o' God sayin', "This hain't wuth nothin' t' Me. Git ye back t' hum!" I got afeered o' that voice an' I lit out back t' hum here, leavin' my claim an' crops t' whoever'd a mind t' take 'em. Ay-eh. I actooly give up what was rightful mine! God's hard, not easy! God's in the stones! Build My church on a rock – out o' stones an' I'll be in them. That's what He meant t' Peter! (*He sighs heavily – a pause.*) Stones. I picked 'em up an' piled 'em into walls. Ye kin read the years o' my life in them walls, every day a hefted stone, climbin' over the hills up and down, fencing in the fields that was mine, whar I'd made thin's grow out o' nothin' – like the will o' God, like the servant o' His hand. It wa'n't easy. It was hard an' He made me hard fur it. (*He pauses.*) All the time I kept gittin' lonesomer. I tuk a wife. She bore Simeon an' Peter. She was a good woman. She wuked hard. We was married twenty year. She never knowed me. She helped, but she never knowed what she was helpin'. I was allus lonesome. She died. After that it wa'n't so lonesome fur a spell. (*A pause.*) I lost count o' the years. I had no time t' fool away countin' 'em. Sim an' Peter

helped. The farm growed. It was all mine! When I thought o'
that I didn't feel lonesome. (*A pause.*) But ye can't hitch yer
mind t' one thin' day an' night. I tuk another wife – Eben's
Maw. Her folks was contestin' me at law over my deeds t' the
farm – my farm! That's why Eben keeps a-talking his fool talk o'
this bein' his Maw's farm. She bore Eben. She was purty – but
soft. She tried t' be hard. She couldn't. She never knowed me
nor nothin'. It was lonesomer 'n hell with her. After a matter o'
sixteen odd years, she died. (*A pause.*) I lived with the boys. They
hated me 'cause I was hard. I hated them 'cause they was soft.
They coveted the farm without knowin' what it meant. It made
me bitter 'n wormwood. It aged me - them coveting what I'd
made fur mine. Then this spring the call come – the voice o'
God's cryin' in my wilderness, in my lonesomeness – t' go out
an' seek an find! (*Turning to her with strange passion.*) I sought ye
an' I found ye! Yew air my Rose o' Sharon! Yer eyes air like. . .
(*She has turned a blank face, resentful eyes to his. He stares at her for a
moment – then harshly.*) Air ye any the wiser fur all I've told ye?

ABBIE (*confusedly*). Mebbe.

CABOT (*pushing her away from him – angrily*). Ye don't know nothin'
– nor never will. If ye don't hev a son t' redeem ye . . . (*This in a
tone of cold threat.*)

ABBIE (*resentfully*). I've prayed, hain't I?

CABOT (*bitterly*). Pray again – fur understandin'!

ABBIE (*a veiled threat in her tone*). Ye'll have a son out o' me I
promise ye.

CABOT. How can ye promise?

ABBIE. I got second-sight, mebbe. I kin foretell. (*She gives a queer
smile.*)

CABOT. I believe ye have. Ye give me the chills sometimes. (*He
shivers.*) It's cold in this house. It's oneasy. They's thin's pokin'
about in the dark in the corners. (*He pulls on his trousers, tucking
in his night-shirt, and pulls on his boots.*)

ABBIE (*surprised*). Whar air ye goin'?

CABOT (*queerly*). Down whar it's restful – whar it's warm – down t'
the barn (*Bitterly.*) I kin talk t' the cows. They know. They know
the farm an' me. They'll give me peace. (*He turns to go out the
door.*)

ABBIE (*a bit frightenedly*). Air ye ailin' to-night, Ephraim?

CABOT. Growin'. Growin' ripe on the bough. (*He turns and goes,
his boots clumping down the stairs. EBEN sits up with a start,*

listening. ABBIE *is conscious of his movement and stares at the wall.*
CABOT *comes out of the house around the corner and stands by the
gate blinking at the sky. He stretches up his hands in a tortured
gesture.)* God A'mighty, call from the dark!

*He listens as if expecting an answer. Then his arms drop, he shakes his
head and plods off toward the barn.* EBEN *and* ABBIE *stare at each
other through the wall.* EBEN *sighs heavily and* ABBIE *echoes it. Both
become terribly nervous, uneasy. Finally* ABBIE *goets up and listens,
her ear to the wall. He acts as if he saw every move she was making; he
becomes resolutely still. She seems driven into a decision – goes out the
door in rear determinedly. His eyes follow her. Then as the door of his
room is opened softly, he turns away, waits in an attitude of strained
fixity.* ABBIE *stands for a second staring at him, her eyes burning with
desire. Then with a little cry she runs over and throws her arms about
his neck, she pulls his head back and covers his mouth with kisses. At
first, he submits dumbly; then he puts his arms about her neck and
returns her kisses, but finally, suddenly aware of his hatred, he hurls her
away from him, springing to his feet. They stand speechless and
breathless, panting like two animals.*

ABBIE (*at last – painfully*). Ye shouldn't, Eben – ye shouldn't – I'd
make ye happy!

EBEN (*harshly*). I don't want happy – from yew!

ABBIE (*helplessly*). Ye do, Eben! Ye do! Why d'ye lie?

EBEN (*viciously*). I don't take t' ye, I tell ye! I hate the sight o' ye!

ABBIE (*with an uncertain troubled laugh*). Waal, I kissed ye anyways –
an' ye kissed back – yer lips was burnin' – ye can't lie 'bout that!
(*Intensely.*) If ye don't care, why did ye kiss me back – why was
yer lips burnin'?

EBEN (*wiping his mouth*). It was like pizen on 'em. *(Then tauntingly.)*
When I kissed ye back, mebbe I thought 'twas someone else.

ABBIE (*wildly*). Min?

EBEN. Mebbe.

ABBIE (*torturedly*). Did ye go t' see her? Did ye r'ally go? I thought
ye mightn't. Is that why ye throwed me off jest now?

EBEN (*sneeringly*). What if it be?

ABBIE (*raging*). They ye're a dog, Eben Cabot!

EBEN (*threateningly*). Ye can't talk that way t' me!

ABBIE (*with a shrill laugh*). Can't I? Did ye think I was in love with ye
– a weak thin' like yew? Not much! I on'y wanted ye fur a purpose
o' my own – an' I'll hev ye fur it yet 'cause I'm stronger'n yew be!

EBEN (*resentfully*). I knowed well it was on'y part o' yer plan t' swaller everythin'!

ABBIE (*tauntingly*). Mebbe!

EBEN (*furious*). Git out o' my room!

ABBIE. This air my room an' ye're on'y hired help!

EBEN (*threateningly*). Git out afore I murder ye!

ABBIE (*quite confident now*). I hain't a mite afeerd. Ye want me, don't ye? Yes, ye do! An yer Paw's son'll never kill what he wants! Look at yer eyes! They's lust fur me in 'em, burnin' 'em up! Look at yer lips now! They're tremblin' an' longin' t' kiss me, an' yer teeth t' bite! (*He is watching her now with a horrible fascination. She laughs a crazy triumphant laugh.*) I'm a-goin' t' make all o' this hum my hum! They's one room hain't mine yet, but it's a-goin' t' be tonight. I'm a-goin' down now an' light up! (*She makes him a mocking bow.*) Won't ye come courtin' me in the best parlour, Mister Cabot?

EBEN (*staring at her – horribly confused – dully*). Don't ye dare! It hain't been opened since Maw died an' was laid out thar! Don't ye . . . (*But her eyes are fixed on his so burningly that his will seems to wither before hers. He stands swaying toward her helplessly.*)

ABBIE (*holding his eyes and putting all her will into her words as she backs out the door*). I'll expect ye afore long, Eben.

EBEN (*stares after her for awhile, walking toward the door. a light appears in the parlour window. He murmurs.*) In the parlour? (*This seems to cause connections, for he comes back and puts on hsi white shirt, collar, half ties the tie mechanically, puts on coat, takes his hat, stands barefooted looking about him in bewilderment, mutters wonderingly.*) Maw! Whar air yew? (*Then goes slowly toward the door in rear.*)

Scene Three

A few minutes later. The interior of the parlour is shown. A grim, repressed room like a tomb in which the family has been interred alive. ABBIE sits on the edge of the horsehair sofa. She has lighted all the candles and the room is revealed in all its preserved ugliness. A change has come over the woman. She looks awed and frightened now, ready to run away.

The door is opened and EBEN appears. His face wears an expression of obsessed confusion. He stands staring at her, his arms hanging disjointedly from his shoulders, his feet bare, his hat in his hand.

ABBIE (*after a pause – with a nervous, formal politeness*). Won't ye set?

EBEN (*dully*). Ay-eh. (*Mechanically he places his hat carefully on the floor near the door and sits stiffly beside her on the edge of the sofa. A pause. They both remain rigid, looking straight ahead with eyes full of fear.*)

ABBIE. When I fust come in – in the dark – they seemed somethin' here.

EBEN (*simply*). Maw.

ABBIE. I kin still feel – somethin' –

EBEN. It's Maw.

ABBIE. At fust I was feered o' it. I wanted t' yell an' run. Now – since yew come – seems like it's growin' soft an' kind t' me. (*addressing the air – queerly.*) Thank yew.

EBEN. Maw allus loved me.

ABBIE. Mebbe it knows I love ye, too. Mebbe that makes it kind t' me.

EBEN (*dully*). I dunno. I should think she'd hate ye.

ABBIE (*with certainty*). No. I kin feel it don't– not no more.

EBEN. Hate ye fur stealin' her place – here in her hum – settin' in her parlour whar she was laid . . . (*He suddenly stops, staring stupidly before him.*)

ABBIE. What is it, Eben?

EBEN (*in a whisper*). Seems like Maw didn't want me t' remind ye.

ABBIE (*excitedly*). I knowed, Eben! It's kind t' me! It don't b'ar me no grudges fur what I never knowed an' couldn't help!

EBEN. Maw b'ars him a grudge.

ABBIE. Waal, so does all o' us.

EBEN. Ay-eh. (*With passion.*) I does, by God!

ABBIE (*taking one of his hands in hers and patting it*). Thar! Don't git riled thinkin' o' him. Think o' yer Maw who's kind t' us. Tell me about yer Maw, Eben.

EBEN. They hain't nothin' much . . . She was kind. She was good.

ABBIE (*putting one arm over his shoulder. He does not seem to notice – passionately*). I'll be kind an' good t' ye!

EBEN. Sometimes she used t' sing fur me.

ABBIE. I'll sing fur ye!

EBEN. This was her hum. This was her farm.

ABBIE. This is my hum. This is my farm.

EBEN. He married her t' steal 'em. She was soft an' easy. He couln't 'preciate her.

ABBIE. He can't 'preciate me!

EBEN. He murdered her with his hardness.

ABBIE. He's murderin' me!

EBEN. She died. (*A pause.*) Sometimes she used to sing fur me. (*He bursts into a fit of sobbing.*)

ABBIE (*both her arms around him – with wild passion*). I'll sing fur ye! I'll die fur ye! (*In spite of her overwhelming desire for him, there is a sincere maternal love in her manner and voice – a horribly frank mixture of lust and mother-love.*) Don't cry, Eben! I'll take yer Maw's place! I'll be everythin' she was t' ye! Let me kiss ye, Eben! (*She pulls his head around. He makes a bewildered pretence of resistance. She is tender.*) Don't be afeered! I'll kiss ye pure, Eben – same's if I was a Maw t' ye – an' ye kin kiss me back 's if yew was my son – my boy – sayin' good night t' me! Kiss me, Eben. (*They kiss in restrained fashion. Then suddenly wild passion overcomes her. She kisses him lustfully again and again and he flings his arms about her and returns her kisses. Suddenly, as in the bedroom, he frees himself from her violently and springs to his feet. He is trembling, all over, in a strange state of terror. ABBIE strains her arms toward him with fierce pleading.*) Don't ye leave me, Eben! Can't ye see it hain't enuf – lovin' ye like a Maw – can't ye see it's got t' be that an' more – much more – a hundred times more – fur me t' be happy – fur yew t' be happy!

EBEN (*to the presence he feels in the room*). Maw! Maw! What d'ye want? What air ye tellin' me?

ABBIE. She's tellin' ye t' love me. She knows I love ye an' I'll be good t' ye. Can't ye feel it? Don't ye know? She's tellin ye t' love me, Eben!

EBEN. Ay-eh. I feel – mebbe she – but – I can't figger out – why – when ye've stole her place – here in her hum – in the parlour whar she was . . .

ABBIE (*fiercely*). She knows I love ye!

EBEN (*his face suddenly lighting up with a fierce triumphant grin*). I see it! I sees why. It's her vengeance on him – so's she kin rest quiet in her grave!

ABBIE (*wildly*). Vengeance o' her on him! Vengeance o' her on me – an' mine on yew – an' yourn on me - an' ourn on him! Vengeance o' God on the hull o' us! What d' we give a durn? I love ye Eben! God knows I love ye! (*She stretches out her arms for him.*)

EBEN (*throws himself on his knees beside the sofa and grabs her in his arms – releasing all his pent-up passion*). An' I Love yew, Abbie! – now I kin say it! I been dyin' fur want o' ye – every hour – since ye come! I love ye! (*Their lips meet in a fierce, bruising kiss.*)

Scene Four

Exterior of the farm-house. It is just dawn. The front door at right is opened and EBEN comes out and walks around to the gate. He is dressed in his working clothes. He seems changed. His face wears a bold and confident expression, he is grinning to himself with evident satisfaction. As he gets near the gate, the window of the parlour is heard opening and the shutters are flung back and ABBIE sticks her head out. Her hair tumbles over her shoulders in disarray, her face is flushed, she looks at EBEN with tender, languorous eyes and calls softly.

ABBIE. Eben. (*As he turns – playfully*). Jest one more kiss afore ye go. I'm goin' t' miss ye fearful all day.

EBEN. An me yew, ye kin bet! (*He goes to her. They kiss several times. He draws away, laughingly.*) Thar. That's enuf, hain't it? Ye won't hev none left fur next time.

ABBIE. I got a million 'on 'em left fur ye! (*Then a bit anxiously.*) D'ye r'ally love me, Eben?

EBEN (*emphatically*). I like ye better'n any gal I ever knowed! That's gospel!

ABBIE. Likin' hain't lovin'.

EBEN. Waal then – I love ye. Now air yew satisfied?

ABBIE. Ay-eh, I be. (*She smiles at him adoringly*).

EBEN. I better git t' the barn. The old critter's liable t' suspicion an' come sneakin' up.

ABBIE (*with a confident laugh*). Let him! I kin allus pull the wool over his eyes. I'm goin' t' leave the shutters open and let in the sun 'n air. This room's been dead long enuf. Now it's goin' t' be my room.

EBEN (*frowning*). Ay-eh.

ABBIE (*hastily*). I meant – our room.

EBEN. Ay-eh.

ABBIE. We made it our'n last night, didn't we? We give it life – our lovin' did. (*A pause.*)

EBEN (*with a strange look*). Maw's gone back t' her grave. She kin sleep now.

ABBIE. May she rest in peace! (*Then tenderly rebuking.*) Ye oughtn't t' talk o' sad thin's – this mornin'.

EBEN. It jest come up in my mind o' itself.

ABBIE. Don't let it. (*He doesn't answer. She yawns.*) Waal, I'm a-goin' t' steal a wink o' sleep. I'll tell the Old Man I hain't feelin' pert. Let him git his own vittles.

EBEN. I see him comin' from the barn. Ye better look smart an' git upstairs.

ABBIE. Ay-eh. Goodbye. Don't ferget me.

She throws him a kiss. He grins — then squares his shoulders and awaits his father confidently. CABOT *walks slowly up from the left, staring up at the sky with a vague face.*

EBEN (*jovially*). Mornin', Paw. Star-gazin' in daylight?

CABOT. Purty, hain't it?

EBEN (*looking around him possessively*). It's a durned purty farm.

CABOT. I mean the sky.

EBEN (*grinning*). How d'ye know? Them eyes o' your'n can't see that fur. (*This tickles his humour and he slaps his thigh and laughs.*) Ho-ho! That's a good un!

CABOT (*grimly sarcastic*). Ye're feelin' right chipper, hain't ye? Whar'd ye steal the likker?

EBEN (*good naturedly*). 'Tain't likker. Jest life. (*Suddenly holding out his hand – soberly.*) Yew 'n' me is quits. Lets shake hands.

CABOT (*suspiciously*). What's come over ye?

EBEN. Then don't. Mebbe it's jest as well. (*A moment's pause.*) What's come over me? (*Queerly.*) Didn't ye feel her passin' – goin' back t' her grave?

CABOT (*dully*). Who?

EBEN. Maw. She kin rest now an' sleep content. She's quits with ye.

CABOT (*confusedly*). I rested. I slept good – down with the cows. They know how t' sleep. They're teachin me.

EBEN (*suddenly jovial again*). Good fur the cows! Waal – ye better git t' work.

CABOT (*grimly amused*). Air yew bossin' me, ye calf?

EBEN (*beginning to laugh*). Ay-eh! I'm bossin' yew! Ha-ha-ha! See
   how ye like it! Ha-ha-ha! I'm the prize rooster o' this roost. Ha-
   ha-ha! (*He goes off toward the barn laughing.*)

CABOT (*looks after him with scornful pity*). Soft-headed. Like his
   Maw. Dead spit 'n' image. No hope in him! (*He spits with
   contemptuous disgust.*) A born fool! (*Then matter-of-factly.*) Waal –
   I'm gittin' peckish. (*He goes toward door.*)

PART THREE

Scene One

A night in late spring the following year. The kitchen and the two bedrooms upstairs are shown. The two bedrooms are dimly lighted by a tallow candle in each. EBEN is sitting on the side of the bed in his room, his chin propped on his fists, his face a study of the struggle he is making to understand his conflicting emotions. The noisy laughter and music from below where a kitchen dance is in progress annoy and distract him. He scowls at the floor.

In the next room a cradle stands beside the double bed.

In the kitchen all is festivity. The stove has been taken down to give more room to the dancers. The chairs, with wooden benches added, have been pushed back against the walls. On these are seated, squeezed in tight against one another, farmers and their wives and their young folks of both sexes from the neighbouring farms. They are all chattering and laughing loudly. They evidently have some secret joke in common. There is no end of winking, of nudging, of meaning nods of the head toward CABOT who, in a state of extreme hilarious excitement increased by the amount he has drunk, is standing near the rear door where there is a small keg of whisky and serving drinks to all the men. In the left corner, front, dividing the attention with her husband, ABBIE is sitting in a rocking chair, a shawl wrapped about her shoulders. She is very pale, her face is thin and drawn, her eyes are fixed anxiously on the open door in rear as if waiting for someone.

The musician is tuning up his fiddle, seated in the far right corner. He is a lanky young fellow with a long weak face. His pale eyes blink incessantly and he grins about him slyly with a greedy malice.

ABBIE (*suddenly turning to a young girl on her right*). Whar's Eben?

YOUNG GIRL (*eyeing her scornfully*). I dunno, Mrs Cabot. I hain't seen Eben in ages. (*Meaningly.*) Seems like he's spent most o' his time t' hum since yew come.

ABBIE (*vaguely*). I tuk his Maw's place.

YOUNG GIRL. Ay-eh. So I've heerd.

She turns away to retail this bit of gossip to her mother sitting next to her. ABBIE turns to her left to a big stoutish middle-aged man whose flushed face and starting eyes show the amount of 'likker' he has consumed.

ABBIE. Ye hain't seen Eben, hev ye?

MAN. No, I hain't. (*Then he adds with a wink.*) If yew hain't, who would?

ABBIE. He's the best dancer in the county. He'd ought t' come an' dance.

MAN (*with a wink*). Mebbe he's doin' the dutiful an' walkin the kid t' sleep. It's a boy, hain't it?

ABBIE (*nodding vaguely*). Ay-eh – born two weeks back - purty's a picter –

MAN. They all is – t' their Maws. (*Then in a whisper with a nudge and a leer.*) Listen, Abbie – if ye ever git tired o' Eben, remember me! Don't fergit now! (*He looks at her uncomprehending face for a second – then grunts disgustedly.*) Waal – guess I'll likker agin. (*He goes over and joins* CABOT *who is arguing noisily with an old farner over cows. They all drink.*)

ABBIE (*this time appealing to nobody in particular*). Wonder what Eben's a-doin'? (*Her remark is repeated down the line with many a guffaw and titter until it reaches the fiddler. He fastens his blinking eyes on* ABBIE.)

FIDDLER (*raising his voice*). Bet I kin tell ye, Abbie, what Eben's doin'! He's down t' the church offerin' up prayers o' thanksgivin'. (*They all titter expectantly.*)

A MAN. What fur? (*Another titter.*)

FIDDLER. 'Cause unto him a – (*He hesitates just long enough.*) – brother is born!

A roar of laughter. They all look from ABBIE *to* CABOT. *She is oblivious, staring at the door.* CABOT, *although he hasn't heard the words, is irritated by the laughter, and steps forward, glaring about him. There is an immediate silence.*

CABOT. What're ye all bleatin' about – like a flock o' goats? Why don't ye dance, damn ye? I axed ye here t' dance – t' eat, drink an' be merry – an' thar ye set caclin' like a lot o' wet hens with the pip! Ye've swilled my likker an' guzzled my vittles like hogs, hain't ye? Then dance fur me, can't ye? That's fa'r an' squa'r, hain't it? (*A grumble of resentment goes around, but they are all evidently in too much awe of him to express it openly.*)

FIDDLER (*slyly*). We're waitin' fur Eben. (*A suppressed laugh.*)

CABOT (*with a fierce exultation*). T' hell with Eben! Eben's done fur now! I got a new son! (*His mood switching with drunken suddenness.*) But ye needn't t' laugh at Eben, none o' ye! He's my blood, if he be a dumb fool. He's better nor any o' yew! He

kin do a day's work a'most up t' what I kin – an' that'd put any
o' yew pore critters t' shame!

FIDDLER. An' he kin do a good night's work, too! (*A roar of
laughter.*)

CABOT. Laugh, ye damn fools! Ye're right just the same, Fiddler.
He kin work day an' night, too, like I kin, if need be!

OLD FARMER (*from behind the keg where he is weaving drunkenly back
and forth – with great simplicity.*) They hain't many t' touch ye,
Ephraim – a son at seventy-six. That's a hard man fur ye! I be
on'y sixty-eight an' I couldn't do it. (*A roar of laughter, in which
CABOT joins uproariously.*)

CABOT (*slapping him on the back*). I'm sorry fur ye, Hi. I'd never
suspicion sech weakness from a boy like yew!

OLD FARMER. An' I never reckoned yew had it in ye nuther,
Ephraim. (*Another laugh.*)

CABOT (*suddenly grim*). I got a lot in me – a hell of a lot – folks
don't know on. (*Turning to the fiddler.*) Fiddle 'er up, durn ye!
Give 'em somethin' t' dance t'! What air ye, an ornament?
Hain't this a celebration? Then grease yer elbow an' go it!

FIDDLER (*seizes a drink which the OLD FARMER holds out to him and
downs it*). Here goes!

He starts to fiddle 'Lady of the Lake'. *Four young fellows and four
girls form in two lines and dance a square dance. The* FIDDLER
*shouts directions for the diferent movements, keeping his words in the
rhythm of the music and interspersing them with jocular personal
remarks to the dancers themselves. The people seated along the walls
stamp their feet and slap their hands in unison.* CABOT *is especially
active in this respect. Only* ABBIE *remains apathetic, staring at the
door as if she were alone in a silent room.*

FIDDLER. Swing your partner t' the right! That's it, Jim! Give her a
b'ar hug! Her Maw hain't lookin'! (*Laughter.*) Change partners!
That suits ye, don't it, Essie, now ye got Reub afore ye? Look at
her redden up, will ye? Waal life is short an' so's love, as the
feller says. (*Laughter.*)

CABOT (*excitedly, stamping his foot*). Go it, boys! Go it, gals!

FIDDLER (*with a wink at the others*). Ye're the spryest seventy-six
ever I sees, Ephraim! Now, if ye'd on'y good eyesight. . .!
(*Suppressed laughter. He gives* CABOT *no chance to retort, but roars.*)
Promenade! Ye're walkin' like a bride down the aisle, Sarah!
Waal, while they's life they's allus hope, I've heerd tell. Swing
your partner to the left! Gosh A'mighty, look at Johnny Cook
high-steppin'! They hain't goin' t' be much strength left fur

howin' in the corn lot t'-morrow. (*Laughter*).

CABOT. Go it! Go it! (*Then suddenly, unable to restrain himself any longer, he prances into the midst of the dancers, scattering them, waving his arms about wildly.*) Ye're all hoofs! Git out o' my road! Give me room! I'll show ye dancin'. Ye're all too soft! (*He pushes them roughly away. They crowd back toward the walls, muttering, looking at him resentfully.*)

FIDDLER (*jeeringly*). Go it Ephraim! Go it! (*He starts 'Pop Goes the Weasel', increasing the tempo with every verse until at the end he is fiddling crazily as fast as he can go.*)

CABOT (*starts to dance, which he does very well and with tremendous vigour. Then he begins to improvise, cuts incredibly grotesque capers, leaping up and cracking his heels together, prancing around in a circle with body bent in an Indian war dance, then suddenly straightening up and kicking as high as he can with both legs. He is like a monkey on a string. And all the while he intersperses his antics with shouts and derisive comments*). Whoop! Here's dancin' fur ye! Whoop! See that! Seventy-six, if I'm a day! Hard as iron yet! Beatin' the young 'uns like I allus done! Look at me! I'd invite ye t' dance on my hundredth birthday on'y ye'll all be dead by then. Ye're a sickly generation! Yer hearts air pink, not red! Yer veins is full o' mud an' water! I be the on'y man in the county! Whoop! See that! I'm a Injun! I've killed Injuns in the West afore ye was born – an' skulped 'em too! They's a arrer wound on my backside I c'd show ye! The hull tribe chased me. I outrun 'em all – with the arrer stuck in me! An' I tuk vengeance on 'em. Ten eyes fur an eye, that was my motter! Whoop! Look at me! I kin kick the ceilin' off the room! Whoop!

FIDDLER (*stops playing – exhaustedly*). God A'mighty, I got enuf. Ye got the devil's strength in ye.

CABOT (*delightedly*). Did I beat yew, too? Waal, ye played smart. Hev a swig.

He pours whisky for himself and FIDDLER. *They drink. The others watch* CABOT *silently with cold, hostile eyes. There is a dead pause. The* FIDDLER *rests.* CABOT *leans against the keg, panting, glaring around him confusedly. In the room above,* EBEN *gets to his feet and tiptoes out the door in rear, appearing a moment later in the other bedroom. He moves silently, even frightenedly, toward the cradle and stands there looking down at the baby. His face is as vague as his reactions are confused, but there is a trace of tenderness, of interested discovery. At the same moment that he reaches the cradle,* ABBIE *seems to sense something. She gets up weakly and goes to* CABOT.

ABBIE. I'm goin' up t' the baby.

CABOT (*with real solicitation*). Air ye able fur the stairs? D'ye want me t' help ye, Abbie?

ABBIE. No. I'm able. I'll be down agin soon.

CABOT. Don't ye git wore out! He needs ye, remember – our son does! (*He grins affectionately, patting her on the back. She shrinks from his touch.*)

ABBIE (*dully*). Don't – tech me. I'm goin' – up. (*She goes. CABOT looks after her. A whisper goes around the room. CABOT turns. It ceases. He wipes his forehead streamng with sweat. He is breathing pantingly.*)

CABOT. I'm a-goin' out t' git fresh air. I'm feelin' a mite dizzy. Fiddle up thar! Dance, all o' ye! Here's likker fur them as wants it. Enjoy yerselves. I'll be back. (*He goes, closing the door behind him.*)

FIDDLER (*sarcastically*). Don't hurry none on our account! (*A suppressed laugh. He imitates ABBIE*). Whar's Eben? (*More laughter.*)

A WOMAN (*loudly*). What's happened in this house is plain as the nose on yer face! (ABBIE *appears in the doorway upstairs and stands looking in surprise and adoration at* EBEN, *who does not see her.*)

A MAN. Ssshh! He's li'ble t' be listenin' at the door. That'd be like him.

Their voices die to an intensive whispering. Their faces are concentrated on this gossip. A noise as of dead leaves in the wind comes from the room. CABOT *has come out from the porch and stands by the gate, leaning on it, staring at the sky blinkingly.* ABBIE *comes across the room silently.* EBEN *does not notice her until quite near.*

EBEN (*starting*). Abbie!

ABBIE. Ssshh! (*She throws her arms around him. They kiss – then bend over the cradle together.*) Ain't he purty? – dead spit 'n' image o' yew!

EBEN (*pleased*). Air he? I can't tell none.

ABBIE. E-zactly like!

EBEN (*frowningly*). I don't like this. I don't like lettin' on what's mine's his'n. I been doin' that all my life. I'm gittin' t' the end o' b'arin' it!

ABBIE (*putting her finger on his lips*). We're doin' the best we kin. We got t' wait. Somethin's bound t' happen. (*She puts her arms around him.*) I got t' go back.

EBEN. I'm goin out. I can't b'ar it with the fiddle playin' an' the laughin'.

ABBIE. Don't git feelin' low. I love ye, Eben. Kiss me. (*He kisses her. They remain in each other's arms.*)

CABOT (*at the gate, confusedly*). Even the music can't drive it out – somethin' – ye kin feel it droppin' off the elums, climbin' up the roof, sneakin'n down the chimney, pokin' in the corners . . . They's no peace in houses, they's no rest livin' with folks. Somethin's always livin' with ye. (*With a deep sigh.*) I'll go t' the barn an' rest a spell. (*He goes wearily toward the barn.*)

FIDDLER (*tuning up*). Let's celebrate the old skunk gittin' fooled! We kin have some fun now he's went. (*He starts to fiddle* 'Turkey in the Straw'. *There is real merriment now. The young folks get up to dance.*)

Scene Two

A half-hour later – exterior – EBEN *is standing by the gate looking up at the sky, an expression of dumb pain bewildered by itself on his face.* CABOT *appears, returning from the barn, walking wearily, his eyes on the ground. He sees* EBEN *and his whole mood immediately changes. He becomes excited, a cruel, triumphant grin comes to his lips, he strides up and slaps* EBEN *on the back. From within comes the whining of the fiddle and the noise of stamping feet and laughing voices.*

CABOT. So har ye be!

EBEN (*startled, stares at him with hatred for a moment – then dully*). Ay-eh.

CABOT (*surveying him jeeringly*). Why hain't ye been in t' dance? They was all axin' fur ye.

EBEN. Let 'em ax.

CABOT. They's a hull passel o' purty gals –

EBEN. T' hell with 'em!

CABOT. Ye'd ought t' be marryin' one o' em soon.

EBEN. I hain't marryin' no one.

CABOT. Ye might 'arn a share o' a farm that way.

EBEN (*with a sneer*). Like yew did, ye mean? I hain't that kind.

CABOT (*stung*). Ye lie! 'Twas yer Maw's folks aimed t' steal my farm from me.

EBEN. Other folks don't say so. (*After a pause – defiantly.*) An' I got a farm, anyways!

CABOT (*derisively*). Whar?

EBEN (*stamps a foot on the ground*). Har.

CABOT (*throws his head back and laughs coarsely*). Ho-ho! Ye hev, hev ye? Waal, that's a good 'un!

EBEN (*controlling himself – grimly*). Ye'll see.

CABOT (*stares at him suspiciously, trying to make him out – a pause – then with scornful confidence*). Ay-eh. I'll see. So'll ye. It's ye what's blind – blind as a mole underground. (EBEN *suddenly laughs, one short sardonic bark:* 'Ha.' *A pause.* CABOT *peers at him with renewed suspicion.*) What air ye hawin' 'bout? (EBEN *turns away without answering.* CABOT *grows angry.*) God A'mighty, yew air a dumb dunce! They's nothin' in that thick skull o' your'n but noise – like a empty keg it be! (EBEN *doesn't seem to hear.* CABOT's *rage grows.*) Yewr farm! God A'mighty! If ye wa'n't a born donkey ye'd know ye'll never own stick nor stone on it, specially now arter him bein' born. It's his'n, I tell ye – his'n arter I die - but I'll live a hundred jest t' fool ye all – an' he'll be growed then – yewr age a'most! (EBEN *laughs again his sardonic* 'Ha.' *This drives* CABOT *into a fury.*) Ha? Ye think ye kin git 'round that someways, do ye? Waal, it'll be her'n, too – Abbie's – ye won't git 'round her – she knows yer tricks – she'll be too much fur ye – she wants the farm her'n – she was afeerd o' ye – she told me ye was sneakin' 'round tryin' t' make love t' her t' git her on yer side. . . ye. . . ye mad fool, ye! (*He raises his clenched fists threateningly.*)

EBEN (*is confronting him, choking with rage*). Ye lie, ye old skunk! Abbie never said no sech thing!

CABOT (*suddenly triumphant when he sees how shaken* EBEN *is*). She did. An' I says, I'll blow his brains t' the top o' them elums – an' she says no, that hain't sense, who'll ye git t' help ye on the farm in his place – an' then she says you'n me ought t' have a son – I know we kin, she says – an' I says, if we do, ye kin have anythin' I've got ye've a mind t'. An' she says, I wants Eben cut off so's this farm'll be mine when ye die! (*With terrible gloating.*) An' that's what's happened, hain't it? An' the farm's her'n! An' the dust o' the road – that's your'n! Ha! Now who's hawin'?

EBEN (*has been listening, petrified with grief and rage – suddenly laughs wildly and brokenly*). Ha-ha-ha! So that's her sneakin' game – all along! – like I suspicioned at fust – t' swaller it all – an' me, too. . . ! (*Madly.*) I'll murder her! (*He springs toward the porch, but* CABOT *is quicker and gets in between.*)

CABOT. No, ye don't!

EBEN. Git out o' my road!

He tries to throw CABOT *aside. They grapple in what becomes immediately a murderous struggle. The old man's concentrated strength is too much for* EBEN. CABOT *gets one hand on his throat and presses him back across the stone wall. At the same moment,* ABBIE *comes out on the porch. With a stifled cry she runs toward them.*

ABBIE. Eben! Ephraim! (*She tugs at the hand on* EBEN*'s throat.*) Let go, Ephraim! Ye're chokin' him!

CABOT (*removes his hand and flings* EBEN *sideways full length on the grass, gasping and choking. With a cry,* ABBIE *kneels beside him, trying to take his head on her lap, but he pushes her away.* CABOT *stands looking down with fierce triumph*). Ye needn't t've fret, Abbie, I wa'n't aimin' t' kill him. He hain't wuth hangin' fur – not by a hell of a sight! (*More and more triumphantly.*) Seventy-six an' him not thirty yit – an' look whar he be fur thinkin' his Paw was easy! No, by God, I hain't easy! An' him upstairs, I'll raise him t' be like me! (*He turns to leave them.*) I'm goin' in an' dance! – Sing an' celebrate! (*He walks to the porch — then turns with a great grin.*) I don't cal'clate it's left in him, but if he gits pesky, Abbie, ye jest sing out. I'll come a-runnin' an', by the Etarnal, I'll put him across my knee an' birch him! Ha-ha-ha! (*He goes into the house laughing. A moment later his loud* 'Whoop' *is heard.*)

ABBIE (*tenderly*). Eben! Air ye hurt! (*She tries to kiss him, but he pushes her violently away and struggles to a sitting position.*)

EBEN (*gaspingly*). T' hell – with ye!

ABBIE (*not believing her ears*). It's me, Eben – Abbie – don't ye know me?

EBEN (*glowering at her with hatred*). Ay-eh – I know ye – now! (*He suddenly breaks down, sobbing weakly.*)

ABBIE (*fearfully*). Eben – what's happened t' ye – why did ye look at me 's if ye hated me?

EBEN (*violently, between sobs and gasps*). I do hate ye! Ye're a whore — a damn trickin' whore!!

ABBIE (*shrinking back horrified*). Eben! Ye don't know what ye're sayin'!

EBEN (*scrambling to his feet and following her – accusingly*). Ye're nothin' but a stinkin' passel o' lies! Ye've been lyin' t' me every word ye spoke, day an' night, since we fust - done it. Ye've kept sayin' ye loved me . . .

ABBIE (*frantically*). I do love ye! (*She takes his hand, but he flings hers away.*)

EBEN (*unheeding*). Ye've made a fool o' me – a sick, dumb fool – a-purpose! Ye've been on'y playin' yer sneakin', stealin' game all along – gittin' me t' lie with ye so's ye'd hev a son he'd think was his'n, an' makin' him promise he'd give ye the farm and let me eat dust, if ye did git him a son! (*Staring at her with anguished, bewildered eyes.*) They must be a devil livin' in ye! 'Tain't human t' be as bad as that be!

ABBIE (*stunned – dully*). He told yew . . .?

EBEN. Hain't it true? It hain't no good in yew lyin' . . .

ABBIE (*pleadingly*). Eben, listen – ye must listen it was long ago – afore we done nothin' – yew was scornin' me – goin' t' see Min when I was lovin' ye – an' I said it t' him t' git vengeance on ye!

EBEN (*unheedingly. With tortured passion*). I wish ye was dead! I wish I was dead along with ye afore this come! (*Ragingly.*) But I'll git my vengeance too! I'll pray Maw t' come back t' help me – t' put her cuss on yew an' him!

ABBIE (*brokenly*). Don't ye, Eben! Don't ye! (*She throws herself on her knees before him, weeping.*) I didn't mean t' do bad t' ye! Fergive me, won't ye?

EBEN (*not seeming to hear her— fiercely*). I'll git squar' with the old skunk – an' yew! I'll tell him the truth 'bout the son he's so proud o'! Then I'll leave ye here t' pizen each other – with Maw comin' out o' her grave at nights – an I'll go t' the gold-fields o' Californi-a whar Sim an' Peter be. . .

ABBIE (*terrified*). Ye won't – leave me? Ye can't!

EBEN (*with fierce determination*). I'm a-goin', I tell ye! I'll git rich thar an' come back an' fight him fur the farm he stole – an I'll kick ye both out in the road – t' beg an' sleep in the woods – an' yer son along with ye – t' starve an' die! (*He is hysterical at the end.*)

ABBIE (*with a shudder – humbly*). He's yewr son, too, Eben.

EBEN (*torturedly*). I wish he never was born! I wish he'd die this minit! I wish I'd never sot eyes on him! It's him – yew havin' him – a purpose t' steal – that's changed everythin'!

ABBIE (*gently*). Did ye believe I loved ye – afore he come?

EBEN. Ay-eh – like a dumb ox!

ABBIE. An' ye don't believe no more?

EBEN. B'lieve a lyin' thief! Ha!

ABBIE (*shudders – then humbly*). An' did ye really love me afore?

EBEN (*brokenly*). Ay-eh – an'ye was trickin' me!

ABBIE. An'ye don't love me no more!

EBEN (*violently*). I hate ye, I tell ye!

ABBIE. An' ye're truly goin' West – goin t' leave me – all on
account o' him bein' born?

EBEN. I'm a-goin' in the mornin' – or may God strike me t' hell!

ABBIE (*after a pause - with a dreadful cold intensity – slowly*). If that's
what his comin's done t' me – killin' yewr love – takin' ye away –
my on'y joy – the on'y joy I ever knowed – like heaven t' me –
purtier'n heaven – then I hate him, too, even if I be his Maw!

EBEN (*bitterly*). Lies! Ye love him! He'll steal the farm fur ye!
(*Brokenly.*) But 'tain't the farm so much – not no more – it's yew
foolin' me – gitin' me t' love ye – lyin' yew loved me – jest t'
steal . . . !

ABBIE (*distractedly*). He won't steal! I'd kill him fust! I do love ye!
I'll prove t' ye –!

EBEN (*harshly*). 'Tain't no use lyin' no more. I'm deaf t' ye! (*He
turns away.*) I hain't seein' ye agen. Goodbye!

ABBIE (*pale with anguish*). Hain't ye even goin' t' kiss me – not
once – arter all we loved - ?

EBEN (*in a hard voice*). I hain't wantin' t' kiss ye never again! I'm
wantin' t' forgit I ever sot eyes on ye!

ABBIE. Eben! – ye mustn't – wait a spell – I want t' tell ye . . .

EBEN. I'm a-goin' in t' git drunk. I'm a-goin' t' dance.

ABBIE (*clinging to his arm – with passionate earnestness*). If I could
make it – 's if he'd never come up between us – If I could prove
t' ye I wa'n't schemin' t' steal from ye – so's everythin' could be
jest the same with us, lovin' each other jest the same, kissin' an'
happy the same's we've been happy all along – if I could do it -
ye'd love me agen, wouldn't ye? Ye'd kiss me agen? Ye wouldn't
never leave me, would ye?

EBEN (*moved*). I calc'late not. (*Then shaking her hand off his arm –
with a bitter smile.*) But ye hain't God, be ye?

ABBIE (*exultantly*). Remember ye've promised! (*Then with strange
intensity.*) Mebbe I kin do one thin' God does!

EBEN (*peering at her*). Ye're gittin' cracked, hain't ye? (*Then going
towards door.*) I'm a-goin' t' dance.

ABBIE (*calls after him intensely*). I'l prove t' ye! I'll prove I love ye
better'n . . . (*He goes in the door, not seeming to hear. She remains*

standing where she is, looking after him – then she finishes desperately.)
Better'n everythin' else put t'gether!

Scene Three

Just before dawn in the morning – shows the kitchen and CABOT*'s bedroom. In the kitchen, by the light of a tallow candle on the table,* EBEN *is sitting, his chin propped on his hands, his drawn face blank and expressionless. His carpet bag is on the floor beside him. In the bedroom, dimly lighted by a small whale-oil lamp,* CABOT *lies asleep.* ABBIE *is bending over the cradle, listening, her face full of terror, yet with an undercurrent of desperate triumph. Suddenly, she breaks down and sobs, appears about to throw herself on her knees beside the cradle, but the old man turns restlessly, groaning in his sleep, and she controls herself, and shrinking away from the cradle with a gesture of horror, backs swiftly toward the door in rear and goes out. A moment later she comes into the kitchen and, running to* EBEN, *flings her arms about his neck and kisses him wildly. He hardens himself, he remains unmoved and cold, he keeps his eyes straight ahead.*

ABBIE (*hysterically*). I done it, Eben! I told ye I'd do it! I've proved I love ye – better'n everythin' so's ye can't never doubt me no more!

EBEN (*dully*). Whatever ye done, it hain't no good now.

ABBIE (*wildly*). Don't ye say that! Kiss me, Eben, won't ye? I need ye t' kiss me arter what I done! I need ye t' say ye love me!

EBEN (*kisses her without emotion – dully*). That's fur goodbye. I'm, a-goin' soon.

ABBIE. No! No! Ye won't go – not now!

EBEN (*going on with his own thoughts*). I been a-thinkin' – an' I hain't goin' t' tell Paw nothin'. I'll leave Maw t' take vengeance on ye. If I told him, the old skunk'd jest be stinkin' mean enuf to take it out on that baby. (*His voice showing emotion in spite of him.*) An' I don't want nothin' bad t' happen t' him. He hain't t' blame fur yew. (*He adds with a certain queer pride.*) An' he looks like me! An', by God, he's mine! An' some day I'll be a-comin' back an' –

ABBIE (*too absorbed in her own thoughts to listen to him— pleadingly*). They's no cause fur ye t' go now – they's no sense – it's all the same's it was – they's nothin' come b'tween us now – arter what I done!

EBEN (*something in her voice arouses him. He stares at her a bit frightenedly*). Ye look mad, Abbie. What did ye do?

ABBIE. I – I killed him, Eben.

EBEN (*amazed*). Ye killed him?

ABBIE (*dully*). Ay-eh.

EBEN (*recovering from his astonishment – savagely*). An' serves him right! But we got t' do somethin' quick t' make it look 's if the old skunk'd killed himself when he was drunk. We kin prove by 'em all how drunk he got.

ABBIE (*wildly*). No! No! Not him! (*Laughing distractedly.*) But that's what I ought t' done, hain't it? I oughter killed him instead! Why didn't ye tell me?

EBEN (*appalled*). Instead? What d'ye mean?

ABBIE. Not him.

EBEN (*his face grown ghastly*). Not – not that baby!

ABBIE (*dully*). Ay-eh!

EBEN (*falls to his knees as if he'd been struck – his voice trembling with horror*). Oh, God A'mighty! A'mighty God! Maw, whar was ye, why didn't ye stop her?

ABBIE (*simply*). She went back t' her grave that night we fust done it, remember! I hain't felt her about since. (*A pause. EBEN hides his head in his hands, trembling all over as if he had the ague. She goes on dully.*) I left the piller over his little face. Then he killed himself. He stopped breathin'. (*She begins to weep softly.*)

EBEN (*rage beginning to mingle with grief*). He looked like me. He was mine, damn ye!

ABBIE (*slowly and brokenly*). I didn't want t' do it. I hated myself fur doin' it. I loved him. He was so purty – dead spit 'n' image o' yew. But I loved yew more – an' yew was goin' away – far off whar I'd never see ye agen, never kiss ye, never feel ye pressed agin me agen - an' ye said ye hated me fur havin' him – ye said ye hated him an' wished he was dead – ye said if it hadn't been fur him comin' it'd be the same's afore between us.

EBEN (*unable to endure this, springs to his feet in a fury, threatening her, his twitching fingers seeming to reach out for her throat*). Ye lie! I never said – I never dreamed ye'd – I'd cut off my head afore I'd hurt his finger!

ABBIE (*piteously, sinking on her knees*). Eben, don't ye look at me like that – hatin' me – not after what I done fur ye – fur us – so's we could be happy agen –

EBEN (*furiously now*). Shut up, or I'll kill ye! I see yer game now –
the same old sneakin' trick – ye're aimin' t' blame me fur the
murder ye done!

ABBIE (*moaning— puttng her hands over her ears*). Don't ye, Eben!
Don't ye! (*She grasps his legs*).

EBEN (*his mood suddenly changing to horror, shinks away from her*).
Don't ye tech me! Ye're pizen! How could ye – t' murder a pore
little critter. Ye must've swapped yer soul t' hell! (*Suddenly
raging.*) Ha! I kin see why ye done it! Not the lies ye jest told –
but 'cause ye wanted t' steal agen – steal the last thin' ye'd left
me – my part o' him – no, the hull o' him – ye saw he looked
like me – ye knowed he was all mine – an' ye couldn't b'ar it – I
know ye! Ye killed him fur bein' mine! (*All this has driven him
almost insane. He makes a rush past her for the door – then turns —
shaking both fists at her, violently.*) But I'll take vengeance now! I'll
git the Sheriff! I'll tell him everythin'! Then I'll sing, 'I'm off to
Californi-a' an' go – gold Golden Gate – gold sun – fields o'
gold in the West! (*This last he half shouts, half croons incoherently,
suddenly breaking off passionately.*) I'm a-goin' fur the Sheriff t'
come an' git ye! I want ye tuk away, locked up from me! I can't
stand t' luk at ye! Murderer an' thief'r not, ye still tempt me! I'll
give ye up t' the Sheriff!

*He turns and runs out, around the corner of house, panting and
sobbing, and breaks into a swerving sprint down the road.*

ABBIE (*struggling to her feet, runs to the door, calling after him*). I love
ye, Eben! I love ye! (*She stops at the door weakly, swaying, about to
fall.*) I don't care what ye do – if ye'll on'y love me agen! (*She
falls limply to the floor in a faint.*)

Scene Four

*About an hour later. Same as Scene Three. Shows the kitchen and
CABOT's bedroom. It is after dawn. The sky is brilliant with the sunrise.
In the kitchen, ABBIE sits at the table, her body limp and exhausted, her
head bowed down over her arms, her face hidden. Upstairs CABOT is still
asleep, but awakens with a start. He looks toward the window and gives a
snort of surprise and irritation – throws back the covers and begins
hurriedly pulling on his clothes. Without looking behind him, be begins
talking to ABBIE whom he supposes beside him.*

CABOT. Thunder 'n' lightnin', Abbie! I hain't slept this late in fifty
year! Looks 's if the sun was full riz a'most. Must've been the
dancin' an' likker. Must be gittin' old. I hope Eben's t' wuk. Ye

might've tuk the trouble t' rouse me, Abbie. (*He turns — sees no one there — surprised.*) Waal – whar air she? Gittin' vittles, I calc'late (*He tiptoes to the cradle and peers down – proudly.*) Mornin', sonny. Purty's a picter! Sleepin' sound. He don't beller all night like most on 'em. (*He goes quietly out the door in rear – a few moments later enters kitchen – sees* ABBIE *– with satisfaction.*) So thar ye be. Ye got any vittles cooked?

ABBIE (*without moving*). No.

CABOT (*coming to her, almost sympathetically*). Ye feelin' sick?

ABBIE. No.

CABOT (*pats her on shoulder. She shudders*). Ye'd best lie down a spell. (*Half jocularly.*) Yer son'll be needin' ye soon. He'd ought t' wake up with a gnashin' appetite, the sound way he's sleepin'.

ABBIE (*shudders – then in a dead voice*). He hain't never goin' t' wake up.

CABOT (*jokingly*). Takes after me this mornin' I hain't slept so late in -

ABBIE. He's dead.

CABOT (*stares at her – bewilderedly*). What – ?

ABBIE. I killed him.

CABOT (*stepping back from her— aghast*). Air ye drunk – 'r crazy – 'r – ?

ABBIE (*suddenly lifts her head and turns on him – wildly*). I killed him, I tell ye! I smothered him. Go up an' see if ye don't b'lieve me!

CABOT *stares at her a second, then bolts out the rear door, can be heard bounding up the stairs, and rushes into the bedroom and over to the cradle.* ABBIE *has sunk back lifelessly into her former position.* CABOT *puts his hand down on the body in the crib. An expression of fear and horror comes over his face.*

CABOT (*shrinking away – trembling*). God A'mighty! God A'mighty. (*He stumbles out the door – in a short while returns to the kitchen – comes to* ABBIE, *the stunned expression still on his face -- hoarsely.*) Why did ye do it? Why? (*As she doesn't answer, he grabs her violently by the shoulder and shakes her.*) I ax ye why ye done it! Ye'd better tell me 'r -

ABBIE (*gives him a furious push which sends him staggering back and springs to her feet - with wild rage and hatred*). Don't ye dare tech me! What right hev ye' t' question me 'bout him? He wa'n't yewr son! Think I'd have a son by yew? I'd die fust! I hate the sight o' ye an' allus did! It's yew I should've murdered, if I'd had good sense! I hate ye! I love Eben. I did from the fust. An' he was Eben's son – mine an' Eben's – not your'n!

CABOT (*stands looking at her dazedly – a pause – finding his words with an effort - dully*). That was it – what I felt – pokin' round the corners – while ye lied – holdin' yerself from me – sayin' ye'd a'ready conceived . . . (*He lapses into crushed silence – then with a strange emotion.*) He's dead, sart'n. I felt his heart. Pore little critter! (*He blinks back one tear, wiping his sleeve across his nose.*)

ABBIE (*hysterically*). Don't ye! Don't ye! (*She sobs unrestrainedly.*)

CABOT (*with a concentrated effort that stiffens his body into a rigid line and hardens his face into a stony mask – through his teeth to himself*). I got t' be – like a stone – a rock o' jedgment! (*A pause. He gets complete control over himself – harshly.*) If he was Eben's, I be glad he air gone! An' mebbe I suspicioned it all along. I felt they was somethin' onnateral – somewhars – the house got so lonesome – an' cold – drivin' me down t' the barn – t' the beasts o' the field . . . Ay-eh. I must've suspicioned – somethin'. Ye didn't fool me – not altogether, leastways – I'm too old a bird – growin' ripe on the bough . . . (*He becomes aware he is wandering, straightens again, looks at* ABBIE *with a cruel grin.*) So ye'd like t' hev murdered me 'stead o' him, would ye? Waal, I'll live to a hundred! I'll live t' see ye hung! I'll deliver ye up t' the jedgment o' God an' the law! I'll git the Sheriff now. (*Starts for the door.*)

ABBIE (*dully*). Ye needn't. Eben's gone fur him.

CABOT (*amazed*). Eben – gone fur the Sheriff?

ABBIE. Ay-eh.

CABOT. T' inform agen ye?

ABBIE. Ay-eh.

CABOT (*considers this – a pause – then in a hard voice*). Waal, I'm thankful fur him savin' me the trouble. I'll git t' wuk. (*He goes to the door – then turns – in a voice full of strange emotion.*) He'd ought t' been my son, Abbie. Ye'd ought t' loved me. I'm a man. If ye'd loved me, I'd never told no Sheriff on ye, no matter what ye did, if they was t' brile me alive!

ABBIE (*defensively*). They's more to it nor yew know, makes him tell.

CABOT (*dryly*). Fur yewr sake, I hope they be. (*He goes out – comes around to the gate – stares up at the sky. His control relaxes. For a moment he is old and weary. He murmurs despairingly.*) God

A'mighty, I be lonesomer'n ever! (*He hears running footsteps from the left, immediately is himself again. EBEN runs in, panting exhaustedly, wild-eyed and mad-looking. He lurches through the gate. CABOT grabs him by the shoulder. EBEN stares at him dumbly.*) Did ye tell the Sheriff?

EBEN (*nodding stupidly*). Ay-eh.

CABOT (*gives him a push away that sends him sprawling – laughing with withering contempt*). Good fur ye! A prime chip o'yer Maw ye be! (*He goes toward the barn, laughing harshly. EBEN scrambles to his feet. Suddenly CABOT turns – grimly threatening.*) Git off this farm when the Sheriff takes her – or, by God, he'll have t' come back an' git me fur murder, too!

He stalks off. EBEN does not appear to have heard him. He runs to the door and comes into the kitchen. ABBIE looks up with a cry of anguished joy. EBEN stumbles over and throws himself on his knees beside her – sobbing brokenly.

EBEN. Fergive me!

ABBIE (*happily*). Eben! (*She kisses him and pulls his head over against her breast.*)

EBEN. I love ye! Fergive me!

ABBIE (*ecstatically*). I'd fergive ye all the sins in hell fur sayin' that! (*She kisses his head, pressing it to her with a fierce passion of possession.*)

EBEN (*brokenly*). But I told the Sheriff. He's comin fur ye!

ABBIE. I kin b'ar what happens t' me – now!

EBEN. I woke him up. I told him. He says, 'Wait 'till I git dressed.' I was waiting. I got to thinkin' o' yew. I got to thinkin' how I'd loved ye. It hurt like somethin' was bustin' in my chest an' head. I got t' cryin'. I knowed sudden I loved ye yet, an' allus would love ye!

ABBIE (*caressing his hair – tenderly*). My boy, hain't ye?

EBEN. I begun t' run back. I cut across the fields an' through the woods. I thought ye might have time t' run away – with me – an' –

ABBIE (*shaking her head*). I got t' take my punnishment – t' pay fur my sin.

EBEN. Then I want t' share it with ye.

ABBIE. Ye didn't do nothin'.

EBEN. I put it in yer head. I wisht he was dead! I as much as urged ye t' do it!

ABBIE. No. It was me alone!

EBEN. I'm as guilty as yew be! He was the child o' our sin.

ABBIE (*lifting her head as if defying God*). I don't repent that sin. I hain't askin' even God t' fergive that!

EBEN. Nor me – but it led up t' the other – an' the murder ye did, ye did 'count o' me – an' it's my murder, too, I'll tell the Sheriff – an' if ye deny it, I'll say we planned it t'gether – an' they'll all b'lieve me, fur they suspicion everythin' we've done, an' it'll seem likely an' true to 'em. An' it is true – way down – I did help ye – somehow.

ABBIE (*laying her head on his – sobbing*). No! I don't want yew t' suffer!

EBEN. I got t' pay fur my part o' the sin! An' I'd suffer wuss leavin' ye, goin' West, thinkin' o' ye day an' night, bein' out when yew was in . . . (*Lowering his voice.*) 'R bein' alive when yew was dead. (*A pause.*) I want t' share with ye, Abbie – prison 'r death 'r hell 'r anythin'! (*He looks into her eyes and forces a trembling smile.*) If I'm sharin' with ye, I won't feel lonesome, leastways.,

ABBIE (*weakly*). Eben! I won't let ye! I can't let ye!

EBEN (*kissing her – tenderly*). Ye can't he'p yerself. I got ye beat fur once!

ABBIE (*forcing a smile – adoringly*). I hain't beat – s'long's I got ye!

EBEN (*hears the sound of feet outside*). Ssshh! Listen! They've come t' take us!

ABBIE. No, it's him. Don't give him no chance to fight ye, Eben. Don't say nothin' – no matter what he says. An' I won't neither. (*It is* CABOT. *He comes up from the barn in a great state of excitement and strides into the house and then into the kitchen.* EBEN *is kneeling beside* ABBIE, *his arm around her, hers around him. They stare straight ahead.*)

CABOT (*stares at them, his face hard. A long pause – vindictively*). Ye make a slick pair o' murderin' turtle-doves! Ye'd ought t' be both hung on the same limb an' left thar t' swing in the breeze an' rot – a warnin' t' old fools like me t' b'ar their lonesomeness alone – an' fur young fools like ye t' hobble their lust. (*A pause. The excitement returns to his face, his eyes snap, he looks a bit crazy.*) I couldn't work today! I couldn't take no interest. T' hell with the farm! I'm leavin' it! I've turned the cows an' other stock loose! I've druv 'em into the woods whar they kin be free! By freein' 'em, I'm freein' myself! I'm quittin' here today! I'll set fire t' house an' barn an' watch 'em burn, an' I'll leave yer Maw t' haunt the ashes, an' I'll will the fields

back t' God, so that nothin' human kin never touch 'em! I'll be
a-goin to Californi-a–t'jine Simeon an' Peter – true sons o'
mine if they be dumb fools – an' the Cabots 'll find Solomon's
Mines t'gether! (*He suddenly cuts a mad caper.*) Whoop! What was
the song they sung? 'Oh Californi-a! That's the land fur me.'
(*He sings this — then gets on his knees by the floor-board under which
the money was hid.*) An' I'll sail thar on one o' the finest clippers
I kin find! I've got the money! Pity ye didn't know whar this was
hidden so's ye could steal. . . (*He has pulled up the board. He stares
– feels – stares again. A pause of dead silence. He slowly turns,
slumping into a sitting position on the floor, his eyes like those of a dead
fish, his face the sickly green of an attack of nausea. He swallows
painfully several times – forces a weak smile at last.*) So – ye did steal
it!

EBEN (*emotionlessly*). I swapped it t' Sim an' Peter fur their share o'
the farm – t' pay their passage t' Californi-a.

CABOT (*with one sardonic laugh*). Ha! (*He begins to recover. Gets slowly
to his feet – strangely.*) I calc'late God give it to 'em – not yew!
God's hard not easy! Mebbe they's easy gold in the West, but it
hain't God's gold. It hain't fur me. I kin hear His voice warnin'
me agen t' be hard an' stay on my farm. I kin see His hand usin'
Eben t' steal t' keep me from weakness. I kin feel I be in the
palm o' His hand, His fingers guidin' me. (*A pause – then he
mutters sadly.*) It's a-goin t' be lonesomer now that ever it war
afore – an' I'm gittin' old, Lord – ripe on the bough. . . (*Then
stiffening.*) Waal – what d'ye want? God's lonesome, hain't He?
God's hard an' lonesome! (*A pause. The* SHERIFF *wih two* MEN
come up the road from the left. They move cautiously to the door. The
SHERIFF *knocks on it with the butt of his pistol.*)

SHERIFF. Open in the name o' the law! (*They start.*)

CABOT. They've come fur ye. (*He goes to the rear door.*) Come in,
Jim! (*The three men enter.* CABOT *meets them in doorway.*) Jest a
minit. Jim. I got 'em safe here. (*The* SHERIFF *nods. He and his
companions remain in the doorway.*)

EBEN (*suddenly calls*). I lied this mornin', Jim. I helped her do it.
Ye kin take me, too.

ABBIE (*brokenly*). No!

CABOT. Take 'em both. (*He comes forward – stares at* EBEN *with a
trace of grudging admiration.*) Purty good – fur yew! Waal, I got t'
round up the stock. Goodbye.

EBEN. Goodbye.

ABBIE. Goodbye.

CABOT *turns and strides past the men – comes out and around the corner of the house, his shoulders squared, his face stony, and stalks grimly toward the barn. In the meantime the* SHERIFF *and* MEN *have come into the room.*

SHERIFF (*embarrassed*). Waal – we'd best start.

ABBIE. Wait. (*Turns to* EBEN.) I love ye, Eben.

EBEN. I love ye, Abbie. (*They kiss. The three men grin and shuffle embarrassedly.*)

EBEN (*to the* SHERIFF). Now. (*He takes* ABBIE's *hand.*) Come. (*They go out the door in rear, the* MEN *following, and come from the house, walking hand-in-hand to the gate.* EBEN *stops there and points to the sunrise sky.*) Sun's a-risin'. Purty, hain't it?

ABBIE. Ay-eh. (*They both stand for a moment looking up raptly in attitudes strangely aloof and devout.*)

SHERIFF (*looking around at the farm enviously – to his companion*). It's a jim-dandy farm, no denyin'. Wish I owned it!

Curtain.

THE GREAT GOD BROWN

Characters

WILLIAM A. BROWN
HIS FATHER, a contractor
HIS MOTHER
DION ANTHONY
HIS FATHER, a builder
HIS MOTHER
MARGARET
HER THREE SONS
CYBEL
TWO DRAUGHTSMEN ⎱ in Brown's office
A STENOGRAPHER ⎰

Scenes

PROLOGUE

The pier of the Casino. Moonlight in middle June.

ACT ONE

Scene One. Sitting-room, Margaret Anthony's apartment. Afternoon, seven years later.

Scene Two. Billy Brown's office. The same afternoon.

Scene Three. Cybel's parlour. That night.

ACT TWO

Scene One. Cybel's parlour. Seven years later. Dusk.

Scene Two. Drafting-room, William A. Brown's office. That evening.

Scene Three. Library, William A. Brown's home. That night.

ACT THREE

Scene One. Brown's office, a month later. Morning.

Scene Two. Library, Brown's home. That evening.

Scene Three. Sitting-room, Margaret's home. That night.

ACT FOUR

Scene One. Brown's office, weeks later. Late afternoon.

Scene Two. Library, Brown's house, hours later. The same night.

EPILOGUE

The pier of the Casino. Four years later.

PROLOGUE

Scene

A cross-section of the pier of the Casino. In the rear, built out beyond the edge, is a rectangular space with benches on the three sides. A rail encloses the entire wharf at the back.

It is a moonlight night in mid-June. From the Casino comes the sound of the school quartet rendering 'Sweet Adeline' with many ultra-sentimental quavers. There is a faint echo of the ensuing hand-clapping – then nothing but the lapping of ripples against the piles and their swishing on the beach – then footsteps on the boards and BILLY BROWN *walks along from right with his* MOTHER *and* FATHER. *The* MOTHER *is a dumpy woman of forty-five, overdressed in black lace and spangles. The* FATHER *is fifty or more, the type of bustling, genial, successful, provincial business man, stout and hearty in his evening dress.*

BILLY BROWN *is a handsome, tall and athletic boy of nearly eighteen. He is blond and blue-eyed, with a likeable smile and a frank good-humoured face, its expression already indicating a disciplined restraint. His manner has the easy self-assurance of a normal intelligence. He is in evening dress.*

They walk arm in arm, the mother between.

MOTHER (*always addressing the father*). This Commencement dance is badly managed. Such singing! Such poor voices! Why doesn't Billy sing?

BILLY (*to her*). Mine is a regular fog horn! (*He laughs.*)

MOTHER (*to the air*). I had a pretty voice, when I was a girl. (*Then, to the father, caustically.*) Did you see young Anthony strutting around the ballroom in dirty flannel trousers?

FATHER. He's just showing off.

MOTHER. Such impudence! He's as ignorant as his father.

FATHER. The old man's all right. My only kick against him is he's been too damned conservative to let me branch out.

MOTHER (*bitterly*). He has kept you down to his level – out of pure jealousy.

FATHER. But he took me into partnership, don't forget –

MOTHER (*sharply*). Because you were the brains! Because he was afraid of losing you! (*A pause.*)

BILLY (*admiringly*). Dion came in his old clothes for a bet with me. He's a real sport. He wouldn't have been afraid to appear in his pyjamas! (*He grins with appreciation.*)

MOTHER. Isn't the moonlight clear! (*She goes and sits on the centre bench. BILLY stands at the left corner, forward, his hand on the rail, like a prisoner at the bar, facing the judge. His FATHER stands in front of the bench on right. The MOTHER announces, with finality.*) After he's through college, Billy must study for a profession of some sort, I'm determined on that! (*She turns to her husband, defiantly, as if expecting opposition.*)

FATHER (*eagerly and placatingly*). Just what I've been thinking, my dear. Architecture! How's that? Billy a first-rate number-one architect! That's my proposition! What I've always wished I could have been myself. Only I never had the opportunity. But Billy – we'll make him a partner in the firm after. Anthony, Brown *and Son, architects* and builders – instead of *contractors* and builders!

MOTHER (*yearning for the realisation of a dream*). And we won't lay sidewalks – or dig sewers – ever again?

FATHER (*a bit ruffled*). I and Anthony can build anything your pet can draw – even if it's a church. (*Then, selling his idea.*) It's a great chance for him! He'll design – expand us – make the firm famous.

MOTHER (*to the air – musingly*). When you proposed, I thought your future promised success – my future – (*With a sigh.*) – Well, I suppose we've been comfortable. Now, it's his future. How would Billy like to be an architect? (*She does not look at him.*)

BILLY (*to her*). All right, Mother. (*Then sheepishly.*) I guess I've never bothered much about what I'd like to do after college – but architecture sounds all right to me, I guess.

MOTHER (*to the air – proudly*). Billy used to draw houses when he was little.

FATHER (*jubilantly*). Billy's got the stuff in him to win, if he'll only work hard enough.

BILLY (*dutifully*). I'll work hard, Dad.

MOTHER. Billy can do anything!

BILLY (*embarrassed*). I'll try, Mother. (*There is a pause.*)

MOTHER (*with a sudden shiver*). The nights are so much colder than they used to be! Think of it, I once went moonlight bathing in June when I was a girl – but the moonlight was so warm and beautiful in those days, do you remember, Father?

FATHER (*puts his arm around her affectionately*). You bet I do, Mother. (*He kisses her. The orchestra at the Casino strikes up a waltz.*) There's the music. Let's go back and watch the young folks dance. (*They start off, leaving BILLY standing there.*)

MOTHER (*suddenly calls back over her shoulder*). I want to watch Billy dance.

BILLY (*dutifully*). Yes, Mother!

He follows them. For a moment the faint sound of the music and the lapping of waves is heard. Then footsteps again and the three Anthonys come in. First come the FATHER and MOTHER, who are not masked. The FATHER is a tall lean man of fifty-five or sixty, with a grim, defensive face, obstinate to the point of stupid weakness. The MOTHER is a thin, frail, faded woman, her manner perpetually nervous and distraught, but with a sweet gentle face that had once been beautiful. The FATHER wears an ill-fitting black suit, like a mourner. The MOTHER wears a cheap, plain, black dress. Following them, as if he were a stranger, walking alone, is their son, DION. He is about the same height as young BROWN, but lean and wiry, without repose, continually in restless nervous movement. His face is masked. The mask is a fixed forcing of his own face – dark, spiritual, poetic, passionately supersensitive, helplessly unprotected in its childlike, religious faith in life – into the expression of a mocking, reckless, defiant, gaily scoffing and sensual young Pan. He is dressed in a grey flannel shirt, open at the neck, rubber-soled shoes over bare feet, and soiled white flannel trousers. The FATHER strides to the centre bench and sits down. The MOTHER, who has been holding to his arm, lets go and stands by the bench at the right. They both stare at DION, who, with a studied carelessness, takes his place at the rail, where young BROWN had stood. They watch him, with queer, puzzled eyes.

MOTHER (*suddenly – pleading*). You simply must send him to college.

FATHER. I won't. I don't believe in it. Colleges turn out lazy loafers to sponge on their poor old fathers! Let him slave like I had to! That'll teach him the value of a dollar! College'll only ·make him a bigger fool than he is already! I never got above grammar school but I've made money and established a sound business. Let him make a man out of himself like I made of myself!

DION (*mockingly – to the air*). This Mr Anthony is my father, but he only imagines he is God the Father. (*They both stare at him.*)

FATHER (*with angry bewilderment*). What – what – what's that?

MOTHER (*gently remonstrating to her son*). Dion, dear! (*Then to her *husband – tauntingly*.) Brown takes all the credit! He tells every one the success is all due to his energy – that you're only an old stick-in-the-mud!

FATHER (*stung, harshly*). The damn fool! He knows better 'n anyone if I hadn't held him down to common sense, with his crazy wild-cat notions, he'd have had us ruined long ago!

MOTHER. He's sending Billy to college – Mrs Brown just told me – going to have him study architecture afterwards, too, so's he can help expand your firm!

FATHER (*angrily*). What's that? (*Suddenly turns on* DION *furiously*.) Then you can make up your mind to go too! And you'll learn to be a better architect than Brown's boy or I'll turn you out in the gutter without a penny! You hear?

DION (*mockingly – to the air*). It's difficult to choose – but architecture sounds less laborious.

MOTHER (*fondly*). You ought to make a wonderful architect, Dion. You've always painted pictures so well –

DION (*with a start – resentfully*). Why must she lie? Is it my fault? She knows I only try to paint. (*Passionately*.) But I will, some day! (*Then quickly, mocking again*.) On to college! Well, it won't be home, anyway, will it? (*He laughs queerly and approaches them. His* FATHER *gets up defensively.* DION *bows to him*.) I thank Mr Anthony for this splendid opportunity to create myself – (*He kisses his* MOTHER, *who bows with a strange humility as if she were a servant being saluted by the young master – then adds lightly*.) – in my mother's image, so she may feel her life comfortably concluded.

He sits in his FATHER's *place at centre and his mask stares with a frozen mockery before him. They stand on each side, looking dumbly at him.*

MOTHER. (*at last, with a shiver*). It's cold. June didn't use to be cold. I remember the June when I was carrying you, Dion – three months before you were born. (*She stares up at the sky*.) The moonlight was warm, then. I could feel the night wrapped around me like a grey velvet gown lined with warm sky and trimmed with silver leaves!

FATHER (*gruffly – but with a certain awe*). My mother used to believe the full of the moon was the time to sow. She was terrible old-fashioned. (*With a grunt*.) I can feel it's bringing on my rheumatism. Let's go back indoors.

DION (*with intense bitterness*). Hide! Be ashamed! (*They both start and stare at him*.)

FATHER (*with bitter hopelessness. To his wife – indicating their son.*)
Who is he? You bore him!

MOTHER (*proudly*). He's my boy! He's Dion!

DION (*bitterly resentful*). What else, indeed! The identical son.
(*Then, mockingly.*) Are Mr Anthony and his wife going in to
dance! The nights grow cold! The days are dimmer than they
used to be! Let's play hide-and-seek. Seek the monkey in the
moon!

*He suddenly cuts a grotesque caper, like a harlequin, and darts off,
laughing with forced abandon. They stare after him – then slowly
follow. Again there is silence except for the sound of the lapping waves.
Then MARGARET comes in, followed by the humbly worshipping
BILLY BROWN. She is almost seventeen, pretty and vivacious,
blonde, with big romantic eyes, her figure lithe and strong, her facial
expression intelligent but youthfully dreamy, especially now in the
moonlight. She is in a simple white dress. On her entrance, her face is
masked with an exact, almost transparent reproduction of her own
features, but giving her the abstract quality of a Girl instead of the
individual MARGARET.*

MARGARET (*looking upward at the moon and singing in low tone as
they enter*). 'Ah, moon of my delight that knowest no wane!'

BILLY (*eagerly*). I've got that record – John McCormack. It's a
peach! Sing some more. (*She looks upward in silence. He keeps
standing respectfully behind her, glancing embarrassedly toward her
averted face. He tries to make conversation.*) I think the *Rubáiyat's*
great stuff, don't you? I never could memorize poetry worth a
darn. Dion can recite lots of Shelley's poems by heart.

MARGARET (*slowly takes off her mask – to the moon*). Dion! (*A pause.*)

BILLY (*fidgeting*). Margaret!

MARGARET (*to the moon*). Dion is so wonderful!

BILLY (*blunderingly*). I asked you to come out here because I
wanted to tell you something.

MARGARET (*to the moon*). Why did Dion look at me like that? It
made me feel so crazy!

BILLY. I wanted to ask you something, too.

MARGARET. That one time he kissed me – I can't forget it! He was
only joking – but I felt – and he saw and just laughed.

BILLY. Because that's the uncertain part. My end of it is a sure
thing, and has been for a long time, and I guess everybody in
town knows it – they're always kidding me – so it's a cinch you
must know – how I feel about you.

MARGARET. Dion's so different from all the others. He can paint beautifully and write poetry and he plays and sings and dances so marvellously. But he's sad and shy, too, just like a baby sometimes, and he understands what I'm really like inside – and – and I'd love to run my fingers through his hair – and I love him! Yes, I love him! (*She stretches out her arms to the moon.*) Oh, Dion, I love you!

BILLY. I love you, Margaret.

MARGARET. I wonder if Dion – I saw him looking at me again tonight – Oh, I wonder . . . !

BILLY (*takes her hand and blurts out*). Can't you love me? Won't you marry me – after college –

MARGARET. Where is Dion, now I wonder?

BILLY (*shaking her hand in an agony of uncertainty*). Margaret! Please answer me!

MARGARET (*her dream broken, puts on her mask and turns to him – matter-of-factly*). It's getting chilly. Let's go back and dance, Billy.

BILLY (*desperately*). I love you! (*He tries clumsily to kiss her.*)

MARGARET (*with an amused laugh*). Like a brother! You can kiss me if you like. (*She kisses him.*) A big-brother kiss. It doesn't count. (*He steps back crushed, with head bowed. She turns away and takes off her mask – to the moon.*) I wish Dion would kiss me again!

BILLY (*painfully*). I'm a poor boob. I ought to know better. I'll bet I know. You're in love with Dion. I've seen you look at him. Isn't that it?

MARGARET. Dion! I love the sound of it!

BILLY (*huskily*). Well – he's always been my best friend – I'm glad it's him – and I guess I know how to lose – (*He takes her hand and shakes it.*) – so here's wishing you all the success and happiness in the world, Margaret – and remember I'll always be your best friend! (*He gives her hand a final shake – swallows hard – then manfully.*) Let's go back in!

MARGARET (*to the moon – faintly annoyed*). What is Billy Brown doing here? I'll go down to the end of the dock and wait. Dion is the moon and I'm the sea. I want to feel the moon kissing the sea. I want Dion to leave the sky to me. I want the tides of my blood to leave my heart and follow him! (*She whispers like a little girl.*) Dion! Margaret! Peggy! Peggy is Dion's girl – Peggy is Dion's little girl – (*She sings laughingly, elfishly.*) Dion is my Daddy-O! (*She is walking toward the end of the dock, off left.*)

BILLY (*who has turned away*). I'm going. I'll tell Dion you're here.

MARGARET (*more and more strongly and assertively until at the end she is a wife and a mother*). And I'll be Mrs Dion – Dion's wife – and he'll be my Dion – my own Dion – my little boy – my baby! The moon is drowned in the tides of my heart, and peace sinks deep through the sea!

She disappears off left, her upturned unmasked face like that of a rapturous visionary . There is silence again, in which the dance music is heard. Then this stops and Dion comes in. He walks quickly to the bench at centre, and throws himself on it, hiding his masked face in his hands. After a moment, he lifts his head, peers about, listens huntedly, then slowly takes off his mask. His real face is revealed in the bright moonlight, shrinking, shy and gentle, full of a deep sadness.

DION (*with a suffering bewilderment*). Why am I afraid to dance, I who love music and rhythm and grace and song and laughter? Why am I afraid to live, I who love life and the beauty of flesh and the living colours of earth and sky and sea? Why am I afraid to love, I who love love? Why am I afraid, I who am not afraid? Why must I pretend to scorn in order to pity? Why must I hide myself in self-contempt in order to understand? Why must I be so ashamed of my strength, so proud of my weakness? Why must I live in a cage like a criminal, defying and hating, I who love peace and friendship? (*Clasping his hands above in supplication.*) Why was I born without a skin, O God, that I must wear armour in order to touch or to be touched?

(A second's pause of waiting silence – then he suddenly claps his mask over his face again, with a gesture of despair, and his voice becomes bitter and sardonic.) Or rather, Old Greybeard, why the devil was I ever born at all?

Steps are heard from the right. DION stiffens and his mask stares straight ahead. BILLY comes in from the right. He is shuffling along disconsolately. When he sees DION, he stops abruptly and glowers resentfully – but at once the 'good loser' in him conquers this.

BILLY (*embarrassedly*). Hello, Dion. I've been looking all over for you. (*He sits down on the bench at right, forcing a joking tone.*) What are you sitting here for, you nut – trying to get more moon-struck? (*A pause – awkwardly.*) I just left Margaret –

DION (*gives a start – immediately defensively mocking*). Bless you, my children!!

BILLY (*gruffly and slangily*). I'm out of it – she gave me the gate. You're the original white-haired boy. Go on in and win! We've been chums ever since we were kids, haven't we? – and – I'm glad it's you, Dion. (*This huskily – he fumbles for DION's hand and gives it a shake.*)

DION (*letting his hand fall back – bitterly*). Chums? Oh no, Billy Brown would despise me!

BILLY. She's waiting for you now, down at the end of the dock.

DION. For me? Which? Who? Oh no, girls only allow themselves to look at what is seen!

BILLY. She's in love with you.

DION (*moved – a pause – stammers*). Miracle? I'm afraid! (*He chants flippantly.*) I love, thou lovest, he loves, she loves! She loves, she loves – what?

BILLY. And I know damn well, underneath your nuttiness, you're gone on her.

DION (*moved*). Underneath! I love love! I'd love to be loved! But I'm afraid! (*Then aggressively.*) *Was* afraid! Not now! Now I can make love – to anyone! Yes, I love Peggy! Why not? Who is she? Who am I? We love, you love, they love, one loves! No one loves! All the world loves a lover, God loves us all and we love Him! Love is a word – a shameless ragged ghost of a word – begging at all doors for life at any price!

BILLY (*always as if he hadn't listened to what the other said*). Say, let's you and me room together at college –

DION. Billy wants to remain by her side!

BILLY. It's a bet, then! (*Forcing a grin.*) You can tell her I'll see that you behave! (*Turns away.*) So long. Remember she's waiting. (*He goes.*)

DION (*dazedly, to himself*). Waiting – waiting for me! (*He slowly removes his mask. His face is torn and transfigured by joy. He stares at the sky raptly.*) O God in the moon, did you hear? She loves me! I'm not afraid! I am strong! I can love! She protects me! Her arms are softly around me! She is warmly around me! She is my skin! She is my armour! Now I am born – I – the I! – one and indivisible – I who love Margaret! (*He glances at his mask triumphantly – in tones of deliverance.*) You are outgrown! I am beyond you! (*He stretches out his arms to the sky.*) O God, now I believe! (*From the end of the wharf, her voice is heard.*)

MARGARET. Dion!

DION (*raptly*). Margaret!

MARGARET (*nearer*). Dion!

DION. Margaret!

MARGARET. Dion! (*She comes running in, her mask in her hands. He springs toward her with outstretched arms, but she shrinks away with a frightened shriek and hastily puts on her mask.* DION *starts back. She speaks coldly and angrily.*) Who are you? Why are you calling me? I don't know you!

DION (*heart-brokenly*). I love you!

MARGARET (*freezingly*). Is this a joke – or are you drunk?

DION (*with a final pleading whisper*). Margaret! (*But she only glares at him contemptuously. Then with a sudden gesture he claps his mask on and laughs wildly and bitterly.*) Ha-ha-ha! That's one on you, Peg!

MARGARET (*with delight, pulling off her mask*). Dion! How did you ever – why, I never knew you!

DION (*puts his arm around her boldly*). How? It's the moon – the crazy moon – the monkey in the moon – playing jokes on us! (*He kisses her with his masked face with a romantic actor's passion again and again.*) You love me! You know you do! Say it! Tell me! I want to hear! I want to feel! I want to know! I want to want! To want you as you want me!

MARGARET (*in ecstasy*). Oh, Dion, I do! I do love you!

DION (*with ironic mastery – rhetorically*). And I love you! Oh, madly! Oh, for ever and ever, amen! You are my evening star and all my Pleiades! Your eyes are blue pools in which gold dreams glide, your body is a young white birch leaning backward beneath the lips of spring. So! (*He has bent her back, his arms supporting her, his face above hers.*) So! (*He kisses her.*)

MARGARET (*with overpowering passionate languor*). Oh, Dion! Dion! I love you!

DION (*with more and more mastery in his tone*). I love, you love, we love! Come! Rest! Relax! Let go your clutch on the world! Dim and dimmer! Fading out in the past behind! Gone! Death! Now! Be born! Awake! Live! Dissolve into dew – into silence – into night – into earth – into space – into peace – into meaning – into joy – into God – into the Great God Pan! (*While he has been speaking, the moon has passed gradually behind a black cloud, its light fading out. There is a moment of intense blackness and silence. Then the light gradually comes on again.* DION's *voice, at first in a whisper, then increasing in volume with the light, is heard.*) Wake up! Time to get up! Time to exist! Time for school! Time to learn! Learn to pretend! Cover your nakedness! Learn to lie! Learn to keep step! Join the procession! Great Pan is dead! Be ashamed!

MARGARET (*with a sob*). Oh, Dion, I am ashamed.

DION (*mockingly*). Ssshh! Watch the monkey in the moon! See him dance! His tail is a piece of string that was left when he broke loose from Jehovah and ran away to join Charley Darwin's circus!

MARGARET. I know you must hate me now! (*She throws her arms around him and hides her head on his shoulder.*)

DION (*deeply moved*). Don't cry! Don't – ! (*He suddenly tears off his mask – in a passionate agony.*) Hate you? I love you with all my soul! Love me! Why can't you love me, Margaret?

He tries to kiss her but she jumps to her feet with a frightened cry, holding up her mask before her face protectingly.

MARGARET. Don't! Please! I don't know you. You frighten me!

DION (*puts on his mask again – quietly and bitterly*). All's well. I'll never let you see again. (*He puts his arm around her – gently mocking.*) By proxy, I love you. There! Don't cry! Don't be afraid! Dion Anthony will marry you some day. (*He kisses her.*) 'I take this woman –' (*Tenderly joking.*) Hello, woman! Do you feel older by aeons? Mrs Dion Anthony, shall we go in and may I have the next dance?

MARGARET (*tenderly*). You crazy child. (*Then, laughing with joy.*) Mrs Dion Anthony! It sounds wonderful, doesn't it?

They go out as The Curtain Falls.

ACT ONE

Scene One

Scene. *Seven years later.*

The sitting-room of MRS DION ANTHONY's *half of a two-family house in the residential quarter of the town – one of those one-design districts that daze the eye with multiplied ugliness. The four pieces of furniture shown are in keeping – an arm-chair at left, a table with a chair behind it at centre, a sofa at right. The same court-room effect of the arrangement of benches in Act One is held to here. The background is a backdrop on which the rear wall is painted with the intolerable lifeless realistic detail of the stereotyped paintings which usually adorn the sitting-rooms of such houses. It is late afternoon of a grey day in winter.*

DION *is sitting behind the table, staring before him. The mask hangs on his breast below his neck, giving the effect of two faces. His real face has aged greatly, grown more strained and tortured, but at the same time, in some queer way, more selfless and ascetic, more fixed in its resolute withdrawal from life. The mask, too, has changed. It is older, more defiant and mocking, its sneer more forced and bitter, its Pan quality becoming Mephistophelean. It has already begun to show the ravages of dissipation.*

DION (*suddenly reaches out and takes up a copy of the New Testament which is on the table and, putting a finger in at random, opens and reads aloud the text at which it points*). 'Come unto me all ye who are heavy laden and I will give you rest.' (*He stares before him in a sort of trance, his face lighted up from within but painfully confused – in an uncertain whisper.*) I will come – but where are you, Saviour? (*The noise of the outer door shutting is heard.* DION *starts and claps the mocking mask on his face again. He tosses the Testament aside contemptuously.*) Blah! Fixation on old Mamma Christianity! You infant blubbering in the dark, you!

He laughs, with a bitter self-contempt. Footsteps approach. He picks up a newspaper and hides behind it hurriedly. MARGARET *enters. She is dressed in stylish, expensive clothes and a fur coat, which look as if they had been remodelled and seen service. She has grown mature and maternal, in spite of her youth. Her pretty face is still fresh and healthy but there is the beginning of a permanently worried, apprehensive expression about the nose and mouth – an uncomprehending hurt in her eyes.* DION *pretends to be engrossed in his paper. She bends down and kisses him.*

MARGARET (*with a forced gaiety*). Good morning – at four in the afternoon! You were snoring when I left!

DION (*puts his arms around her with a negligent, accustomed gesture – mockingly*). The Ideal Husband!

MARGARET (*already preoccupied with another thought – comes and sits in chair on left*). I was afraid the children would disturb you, so I took them over to Mrs Young's to play. (*A pause. He picks up the paper again. She asks anxiously.*) I suppose they'll be all right over there, don't you? (*He doesn't answer. She is more hurt than offended.*) I wish you'd try to take more interest in the children, Dion.

DION (*mockingly*). Become a father – before breakfast? I'm in too delicate a condition. (*She turns away, hurt. Penitently he pats her hand – vaguely.*) All right. I'll try.

MARGARET (*squeezing his hand – with possessive tenderness*). Play with them. You're a bigger kid than they are – underneath.

DION (*self-mockingly – flipping the Bible*). Underneath – I'm becoming downright infantile! 'Suffer these little ones!'

MARGARET (*keeping to her certainty*). You're my oldest.

DION (*with mocking appreciation*). She puts the Kingdom of Heaven in its place!

MARGARET (*withdrawing her hand*). I was serious.

DION. So was I – about something or other. (*He laughs.*) This domestic diplomacy! We communicate in code – when neither has the other's key.

MARGARET (*frowns confusedly – then forcing a playful tone*). I want to have a serious talk with you, young man! In spite of your promises, you've kept up the hard drinking and gambling you started the last year abroad.

DION. From the time I realised it wasn't in me to be an artist – except in living – and not even in that! (*He laughs bitterly.*)

MARGARET (*with conviction*). But you *can* paint, Dion – beautifully!

DION (*with deep pain*). No! (*He suddenly takes her hand and kisses it gratefully.*) I love Margaret! Her blindness surpasseth all understanding! (*Then bitterly.*) – or is it pity?

MARGARET. We've only got about one hundred dollars left in the bank.

DION (*with dazed surprise*). What? Is all the money from the sale of the house gone?

MARGARET (*wearily*). Every day or so you've been cashing

cheques. You've been drinking – you haven't counted –

DION (*irritably*). I know! (*A pause – soberly*). No more estate to fall
back on, eh? Well, for five years it kept us living abroad in
peace. It bought us a little happiness – of a kind – didn't it? –
living and loving and having children – (*A slight pause – bitterly*).
– thinking one was creating before one discovered one couldn't.

MARGARET (*this time with forced conviction*). But you *can* paint –
beautifully!

DION (*angrily*). Shut up! (*A pause – then jeeringly*.) So my wife thinks
it behoves me to settle down and support my family in the
meagre style to which they'll have to become accustomed?

MARGARET (*shamefacedly*). I didn't say – still – something's got to
be done.

DION (*harshly*). Will Mrs Anthony helpfully suggest what?

MARGARET. I met Billy Brown on the street. He said you'd have
made a good architect, if you'd stuck to it.

DION. Flatterer! Instead of leaving college when my Old Man died?
Instead of marrying Peggy and going abroad and being happy?

MARGARET (*as if she hadn't heard.*) He spoke of how well you used
to draw.

DION. Billy was in love with Margaret at one time.

MARGARET. He wanted to know why you've never been in to see
him.

DION. He's bound heaven-bent for success. It's the will of
Mammon! Anthony and Brown, contractors and builders –
death subtracts Anthony and I sell out – Billy graduates – Brown
and Son, architects and builders – old man Brown perishes of
paternal pride – and now we have William A. Brown, architect!
Why his career itself already has an architectural design! One of
God's mud pies!

MARGARET. He particularly told me to ask you to drop in.

DION (*springs to his feet – assertively*). No! Pride! I have been alive!

MARGARET. Why don't you have a talk with him?

DION. Pride in my failure.

MARGARET. You were always such close friends.

DION (*more and more desperately*). The pride which came after man's
fall – by which he laughs as a creator at his self-defeats!

MARGARET. Not for my sake – but for your own – and, above, all for the children's!

DION (*with terrible despair*). Pride! Pride without which the Gods are worms!

MARGARET (*after a pause, meekly and humbly*). You don't want to? It would hurt you? All right, dear. Never mind. We'll manage somehow – you mustn't worry – you must start your beautiful painting again – and I can get that position in the library – it would be such fun for me working there! . . . (*She reaches out and takes his hand – tenderly.*) I love you, dear. I understand.

DION (*slumps down into his chair, crushed, his face averted from hers, as hers is from him, although their hands are still clasped – in a trembling, expiring voice*). Pride is dying! (*As if he were suffocating, he pulls the mask from his resigned, pale, suffering face. He prays like a Saint in the desert, exorcising a demon.*) Pride is dead! Blessed are the meek! Blessed are the poor in spirit!

MARGARET (*without looking at him – in a comforting motherly tone*). My poor boy!

DION (*resentfully – clapping on his mask again and springing to his feet – derisively*). Blessed are the meek for they shall inherit graves! Blessed are the poor in spirit for they are blind! (*Then with tortured bitterness.*) All right! Then I ask my wife to go and ask Billy Brown – that's more deadly than if I went myself! (*With wild mockery.*) Ask him if he can't find an opening for a talented young man who is only honest when he isn't sober – implore him, beg him in the name of old love, old friendship – to be a generous hero and save the woman and her children! (*He laughs with a sort of diabolical, ironical glee now, and starts to go out.*)

MARGARET (*meekly*). Are you going up street, Dion?

DION. Yes.

MARGARET. Will you stop at the butcher's and ask them to send two pounds of pork chops?

DION. Yes.

MARGARET. And stop at Mrs Young's and tell the children to hurry right home?

DION. Yes.

MARGARET. Will you be back for dinner, Dion?

DION. No. (*He goes, the outer door slams. MARGARET sighs with a tired incomprehension and goes to the window and stares out.*)

MARGARET (*worriedly*). I hope they'll be careful, crossing the street.

Curtain.

Scene Two

Scene. BILLY BROWN's Office, at five in the afternoon. At centre, a fine mahogany desk with a swivel chair behind it. To the left of desk, an office armchair. To the right of desk, an office lounge. The background is a backdrop of an office wall, treated similarly to that of Scene One in its over-meticulous representation of detail.

BILLY BROWN *is seated at the desk looking over a blue print by the light of a desk lamp. He has grown into a fine-looking, well-dressed, capable, college-bred American business man, boyish still and with the same engaging personality.*

The telephone rings.

BROWN (*answering it*). Yes? Who? (*This in surprise – then with eager pleasure.*) Ask her to come right in.

   He gets up and goes to the door, expectant and curious. MARGARET enters. Her face is concealed behind the mask of the pretty young matron, still hardly a woman, who cultivates a naively innocent and bravely hopeful attitude toward things and acknowledges no wound to the world. She is dressed as in Scene One but with an added touch of effective primping here and there.

MARGARET (*very gaily*). Hello, Billy Brown!

BROWN (*awkward in her presence, shakes her hand*). Come in. Sit down. This is a pleasant surprise, Margaret.

   She sits down on the lounge. He sits in his chair behind the desk, as before.

MARGARET (*looking around*). What lovely offices! My, but Billy Brown is getting grand!

BROWN (*pleased*). I've just moved in. The old place was too stuffy.

MARGARET. It looks so prosperous – but then, Billy is doing so wonderfully well, every one says.

BROWN (*modestly*). Well, to be frank, it's been mostly luck. Things have come my way without my doing much about it. (*Then, with an abashed pride.*) Still – I have done a little something myself. (*He picks the plan from the desk.*) See this? It's my design for the New Municipal Building. It's just been accepted – provisionally – by the Committee.

MARGARET (*taking it – vaguely*). Oh? (*She looks at it abstractedly. There is a pause. Suddenly.*) You mentioned the other day how well Dion used to draw –

BROWN (*a bit stiffly*). Yes, he certainly did. (*He takes the drawing from her and at once becomes interested and squints at it frowningly.*)

Did you notice that anything seemed lacking in this?

MARGARET (*indifferently*). Not at all.

BROWN (*with a cheerful grin*). The Committee want it made a little more American. It's too much of a conventional Greco-Roman tomb, they say. (*Laughs.*) They want an original touch of modern novelty stuck in to liven it up and make it look different from other town halls. (*Putting the drawing back on his desk.*) And I've been figuring out how to give it to them, but my mind doesn't seem to run that way. Have you any suggestion?

MARGARET (*as if she hadn't heard*). Dion certainly draws well, Billy Brown was saying?

BROWN (*trying not to show his annoyance*). Why, yes – he did – and still can, I expect. (*A pause. He masters what he feels to be an unworthy pique and turns to her generously.*) Dion would have made a cracking good architect.

MARGARET (*proudly*). I know. He could be anything he wanted to.

BROWN (*a pause – embarrassedly*). Is he working at anything these days?

MARGARET (*defensively*). Oh, yes! He's painting wonderfully! But he's just like a child, he's so impractical. He doesn't try to have an exhibition anywhere, or anything.

BROWN (*surprised*). The one time I ran into him, I thought he told me he'd destroyed all his pictures – that he'd got sick of painting and completely given it up.

MARGARET (*quickly*). He always tells people that. He doesn't want anyone even to look at his things, imagine! He keeps saying they're rotten – when they're really too beautiful! He's too modest for his own good, don't you think? But it is true he hasn't done so much lately since we've been back. You see the children take up such a lot of his time. He just worships them! I'm afraid he's becoming a hopeless family man, just the opposite of what anyone would expect who knew him in the old days.

BROWN (*painfully embarrassed by her loyalty and his knowledge of the facts*). Yes, I know. (*He coughs self-consciously.*)

MARGARET (*aroused by something in his manner*). But I suppose the gossips are telling the same silly stories about him they always did. (*She forces a laugh.*) Poor Dion! Give a dog a bad name! (*Her voice breaks a little in spite of herself.*)

BROWN (*hastily*). I haven't heard any stories – (*He stops uncertainly, then decides to plunge in*). – except about money matters.

MARGARET (*forcing a laugh*). Oh, perhaps they're true enough.

Dion is such a generous fool with his money, like all artists.

BROWN (*with a certain doggedness*). There's a rumour that you've applied for a position at the Library.

MARGARET (*forcing a gay tone*). Yes, indeed! Won't it be fun! Maybe it'll improve my mind! And one of us has got to be practical, so why not me? (*She forces a gay, girlish laugh.*)

BROWN (*impulsively reaches out and takes her hand – awkwardly*). Listen, Margaret. Let's be perfectly frank, will you? I'm such an old friend, and I want like the deuce to . . . You know darn well I'd do anything in the world to help you – or Dion.

MARGARET (*withdrawing her hand, coldly*). I'm afraid I – don't understand, Billy Brown.

BROWN (*acutely embarrassed*). Well, I – I just meant – you know, if you needed – (*A pause. He looks questioningly at her averted face – then ventures on another tack, matter-of-factly.*) I've got a proposition to make to Dion – if I could ever get hold of him. It's this way: business has been piling up on me – a run of luck – but I'm short-handed. I need a crack chief draughtsman darn badly – or I'm liable to lose out. Do you think Dion would consider it – as a temporary stop-gap – until he felt in the painting mood again?

MARGARET (*striving to conceal her eagerness and relief – judicially*). Yes – I really do. He's such a good sport and Billy and he were such pals once. I know he'd be only too tickled to help him out.

BROWN (*diffidently*). I thought he might be sensitive about working for – I mean, with me – when, if he hadn't sold out to Dad he'd be my partner now – (*Earnestly.*) – and, by jingo, I wish he was! (*Then, abruptly.*) Let's try to nail him down right away, Margaret. Is he home now? (*He reaches for the 'phone.*)

MARGARET (*hurriedly*). No, he – he went out for a long walk.

BROWN. Perhaps I can locate him later around town somewhere.

MARGARET (*with a note of pleading*). Please don't trouble. It isn't necessary. I'm sure when I talk to him – he's coming home to dinner – (*Getting up.*) Then it's all settled, isn't it? Dion will be so glad to be able to help an old friend – he's so terribly loyal, and he's always liked Billy Brown so much! (*Holding out her hand.*) I really must go now!

BROWN (*shakes her hand*). Goodbye, Margaret. I hope you'll be dropping in on us a lot when Dion gets here.

MARGARET. Yes. (*She goes.*)

BROWN (*sits at his desk again, looking ahead in a not unsatisfying melancholy reverie. He mutters admiringly but pityingly*). Poor

Margaret! She's a game sport, but it's pretty damn tough on her! (*Indignantly.*) By God, I'm going to give Dion a good talking-to one of these days!

Curtain.

Scene Three

Scene. CYBEL's *parlour. An automatic, penny-in-the-slot player-piano is at centre, rear. On its right is a dirty gilt second-hand sofa. At the left is a bald-spotted crimson plush chair. The backdrop for the rear wall is cheap wall-paper of a dull yellow-brown, resembling a blurred impression of a fallow field in early spring. There is a cheap alarm clock on top of the piano. Beside it her mask is lying.*

DION *is sprawled on his back, fast asleep on the sofa. His mask has fallen down on his chest. His pale face is singularly pure, spiritual and sad.*

The player-piano is groggily banging out a sentimental medley of 'Mother-Mammy' tunes.

CYBEL *is seated on the stool in front of the piano. She is a strong, calm, sensual, blonde girl of twenty or so, her complexion fresh and healthy, her figure full-breasted and wide-hipped, her movements slow and solidly languorous like an animal's, her large eyes dreamy with the reflected stirring of profound instincts. She chews gum like a sacred cow forgetting time with an eternal end. Her eyes are fixed, incuriously, on* DION's *pale face.*

CYBEL (*as the tune runs out, glances at the clock, which indicates midnight, then goes slowly over to* DION *and puts her hand gently on his forehead*). Wake up!

DION (*stirs, sighs and murmurs dreamily*). 'And He laid his hands on them and healed them.' (*Then with a start he opens his eyes and, half sitting up, stares at her bewilderedly.*) What – where – who are you? (*He reaches for his mask and claps it on defensively.*)

CYBEL (*placidly*). Only another female. You was camping on my steps, sound asleep. I didn't want to run any risk getting into more trouble with the cops pinching you there and blaming me, so I took you in to sleep it off.

DION (*mockingly*). Blessed are the pitiful, Sister! I'm broke – but you will be rewarded in Heaven!

CYBEL (*calmly*). I wasn't wasting my pity. Why should I? You were happy, weren't you?

DION (*approvingly*). Excellent! You're not a moralist, I see.

CYBEL (*going on*). And you look like a good boy, too – when you're asleep. Say, you better beat it home to bed or you'll be locked out.

DION (*mockingly*). Now you're becoming maternal, Miss Earth. Is that the only answer – to pin my soul into every vacant diaper? (*She stares down at his mask, her face growing hard. He laughs.*) But please don't stop stroking my aching brow. Your hand is a cool mud poultice on the sting of thought!

CYBEL (*calmly*). Stop acting. I hate ham fats. (*She looks at him as if waiting for him to remove his mask – then turns her back indifferently and goes to the piano.*) Well, if you simply got to be a regular devil like all the other visiting sports, I s'pose I got to play with you. (*She takes her mask and puts it on – then turns. The mask is the rouged and eye-blackened countenance of the hardened prostitute. In a coarse, harsh voice.*) Kindly state your dishonourable intentions, if any! I can't sit up all night keeping company! Let's have some music! (*She puts a plug in the machine. The same sentimental medley begins to play. The two masks stare at each other. She laughs.*) Shoot! I'm all set! It's your play, Kid Lucifer!

DION (*slowly removes his mask. She stops the music with a jerk. His face is gentle and sad - humbly*). I'm sorry. It has always been such agony for me to be touched!

CYBEL (*taking off her mask – sympathetically as she comes back and sits down on her stool*). Poor kid! I've never had one, but I can guess. They hug and kiss you and take you on their laps and pinch you and want to see you getting dressed and undressed – as if they own you – I bet you I'd never let them treat one of mine that way!

DION (*turning to her*). You're lost in blind alleys, too. (*Suddenly holding out his hand to her.*) But you're strong. Let's be friends.

CYBEL (*with a strange sternness, searches his face*). And never nothing more?

DION (*with a strange smile*). Let's say, never anything less!

She takes his hand. There is a ring a the outside door bell. They stare at each other. There is another ring.

CYBEL (*puts on her mask, DION does likewise. Mockingly*). When you got to love to live it's hard to love living. I better join the A.F. of L. and soap-box for the eight-hour night! Got a nickel, baby? Play a tune. (*She goes out. DION puts a nickel in. The same sentimental tune starts. CYBEL returns, followed by BILLY BROWN. His face is rigidly composed, but his superior disgust for DION can be seen. DION jerks off the music and he and BILLY look at each other for a moment, CYBEL watching them both – then, bored, she yawns.*) He's hunting for you. Put out the lights when you go. I'm going to sleep. (*She starts to go – then, as if reminded of something – to*

DION.) Life's all right, if you let it alone. (*Then mechanically flashing a trade smile at* BILLY.) Now you know the way, Handsome, call again! (*She goes.*)

BROWN (*after an awkward pause*). Hello, Dion! I've been looking all over town for you. This place was the very last chance. . . (*Another pause – embarrassedly.*) Let's take a walk.

DION (*mockingly*). I've given up exercise. They claim it lengthens your life.

BROWN (*presuasively*). Come on, Dion, be a good fellow. You're certainly not staying here –

DION. Billy would like to think me taken in *flagrante delicto*, eh?

BROWN. Don't be a damn fool! Listen to me! I've been looking you up for purely selfish reasons. I need your help

DION (*astonished*). What?

BROWN. I've a proposition to make that I hope you'll consider favourably out of old friendship. To be frank, Dion, I need you to lend me a hand down at the office.

DION (*with a harsh laugh*). So it's the job, is it? Then my poor wife did a-begging go!

BROWN (*repelled–sharply*). On the contrary, I had to beg her to beg you to take it! (*More angrily.*) Look here, Dion! I won't listen to you talk that way about Margaret! And you wouldn't if you weren't drunk! (*Suddenly shaking him.*) What in hell has come over you, anyway! You didn't use to be like this! What the devil are you going to do with yourself – sink into the gutter and drag Margaret with you? If you'd heard her defend you, lie about you, tell me how hard you were working, what beautiful things you were painting, how you stayed at home and idolised the children! – when every one knows you've been out every night sousing and gambling away the last of your estate . . . (*He stops, ashamed, controlling himself.*)

DION (*wearily*). She was lying about her husband, not me, you fool! But it's no use explaining. (*Then, in a sudden, excitable passion.*) What do you want? I agree to anything – except the humiliation of yelling secrets at the deaf!

BROWN (*trying a bullying tone – roughly*). Bunk! Don't try to crawl out! There's no excuse and you know it. (*Then as* DION *doesn't reply – penitently.*) But I know I shouldn't talk this way, old man! It's only because we're such old pals – and I hate to see you wasting yourself – you who had more brains than any of us! But, damn it, I suppose you're too much of a rotten cynic to believe I mean what I've just said!

DION (*touched*). I know Billy was always Dion Anthony's friend.

BROWN. You're damn right, I am – and I'd have proved it long
ago if you'd only given me half a chance! After all, I couldn't
keep chasing after you and be snubbed every time. A man has
some pride!

DION (*bitterly mocking*). Dead wrong! Never more! None whatever!
It's unmoral! Blessed are the poor in spirit, Brother! When
shall I report?

BROWN (*eagerly*). Then you'll take the – you'll help me?

DION (*wearily bitter*). I'll take the job. One must do something to
pass away the time, while one is waiting – for one's next
incarnation.

BROWN (*jokingly*). I'd say it was a bit early to be worrying about that.
(*Trying to get DION started.*) Come along, now. It's pretty late.

DION (*shakes his hand off his shoulder and walks away from him – after
a pause*). Is my father's chair still there?

BROWN (*turns away – embarrassed*). I – I don't really remember,
Dion – I'll look it up.

DION (*taking off his mask – slowly*). I'd like to sit where he spun what
I have spent. What aliens we were to each other! When he lay
dead, his face looked so familiar that I wondered where I had
met that man before. Only at the second of my conception. After
that, we grew hostile with concealed shame. And my mother? I
remember a sweet, strange girl, with affectionate, bewildered
eyes as if God had locked her in a dark closet without any
explanation. I was the sole doll our ogre, her husband, allowed
her and she played mother and child with me for many years in
that house until at last through two tears I watched her die with
the shy pride of one who has lengthened her dress and put up
her hair. And I felt like a forsaken toy and cried to be buried
with her, because her hands alone had caressed without clawing.
She lived long and aged greatly in the two days before they
closed her coffin. The last time I looked, her purity had
forgotten me, she was stainless and imperishable, and I knew my
sobs were ugly and meaningless to her virginity; so I shrank away,
back into life, with naked nerves jumping like fleas, and in due
course of nature another girl called me her boy in the moon and
married me and became three mothers in one person, while I
got paint on my paws in an endeavour to see God! (*He laughs
wildly – claps on his mask.*) But that Ancient Humorist had given
me weak eyes, so now I'll have to forswear my quest for Him and
go in for the Omnipresent Successful Serious One, the Great
God Mr Brown, instead! (*He makes him a sweeping, mocking bow.*)

BROWN (*repelled but cajolingly*). Shut up, you nut! You're still drunk. Come on! Let's start! (*He grabs* DION *by the arm and switches off the light.*)

DION (*from the darkness – mockingly*). I am thy shorn, bald, nude sheep! Lead on, Almighty Brown, thou Kindly Light!

Curtain.

ACT TWO

Scene One

Scene. CYBEL*'s parlour – about sunset in spring seven years later. The arrangement of furniture is the same but the chair and sofa are new, bright-coloured, costly pieces. The old automatic piano at centre looks exactly the same. The cheap alarm clock is still on top of it. On either side of the clock, the masks of* DION *and* CYBEL *are lying. The background backdrop is brilliant, stunning wall-paper, on which crimson and purple flowers and fruits tumble over one another in a riotously profane lack of any apparent design.*

DION *sits in the chair on left,* CYBEL *on the sofa. A card-table is between them. Both are playing solitaire.* DION *is now prematurely grey. His face is that of an ascetic, a martyr, furrowed by pain and self-torture, yet lighted from within by a spiritual calm and human kindliness.*

CYBEL *has grown stouter and more voluptuous, but her face is still unmarked and fresh, her calm more profound. She is like an unmoved idol of Mother Earth.*

The piano is whining out its same old sentimental medley. They play their cards intently and contentedly. The music stops.

CYBEL (*musingly*). I love those rotten old sob tunes. They make me wise to people. That's what's inside them – what makes them love and murder their neighbour – crying jags set to music!

DION (*compassionately*). Every song is a hymn. They keep trying to find the Word in the Beginning.

CYBEL. They try to know too much. It makes them weak. I never puzzled over them myself. I gave them a Tart. They understood her and knew their parts and acted naturally. And on both sides we were able to keep our real virtue, if you get me. (*She plays her last card – indifferently.*) I've made it again.

DION (*smiling*). Your luck is uncanny. It never comes out for me.

CYBEL. You keep getting closer, but it knows you still want to win – a little bit – and it's wise all I care about is playing. (*She lays out another game.*) Speaking of my canned music, our Mr Brown hates that old box. (*At the mention of* BROWN, DION *trembles as if suddenly possessed, has a terrible struggle with himself, then while she continues to speak, gets up like an automaton and puts on his mask.*

The mask is now terribly ravaged. All of its Pan quality has changed into a diabolical Mephistophelean cruelty and irony.) He doesn't mind the music inside. That gets him somehow. But he thinks the case looks shabby and he wants it junked. But I told him that just because he's been keeping me so long, he needn't start bossing like a husband or I'll – (*She looks up and sees the masked* DION *standing by the piano – calmly.*) Hello! Getting jealous again?

DION (*jeeringly*). Are you falling in love with your keeper, old Sacred Cow?

CYBEL (*without taking offence*). Cut it! You've been asking me that for years. Be yourself! He's healthy and handsome – but he's too guilty. What makes you pretend you think love is so important, anyway? It's just one of a lot of things you do to keep life living.

DION (*in same tone*). Then you've lied when you've said you loved me, have you, Old Filth?

CYBEL (*affectionately*). You'll never grow up! We've been friends, haven't we, for seven years? I've never let myself want you nor you me. Yes, I love you. It takes all kinds of love to make a world! Ours is the living cream, I say, living rich and high! (*A pause. Coaxingly.*) Stop hiding. I know you.

DION (*taking off his mask, wearily comes and sits down at her feet and lays his head in her lap – with a grateful smile*). You're strong. You always give. You've given my weakness strength to live.

CYBEL (*tenderly, stroking his hair maternally*). You're not weak. You were born with ghosts in your eyes and you were brave enough to go looking into your own dark – and you got afraid. (*After a pause.*) I don't blame your being jealous of Mr Brown sometimes. I'm jealous of your wife, even though I know you do love her.

DION (*slowly*). I love Margaret. I don't know who my wife is.

CYBEL (*after a pause – with a queer broken laugh*). Oh, God, sometimes the truth hits me such a sock between the eyes I can see the stars! – and then I'm so damn sorry for the lot of you, every damn mother's son of a gun of you, that I'd like to run out naked into the street and love the whole moon to death like I was bringing you all a new brand of dope that'd make you forget everything that ever was for good! (*Then, with a twisted smile.*) But they wouldn't see me, any more than they see each other. And they keep right on moving along and dying without my help anyway.

DION (*sadly*). You've given me strength to die.

CYBEL. You may be important but your life's not. There's millions of it born every second. Life can cost too much even for a sucker to afford it – like everything else. And it's not sacred – only the you inside is. The rest is earth.

DION (*gets to his knees and with clasped hands looks up raptly and prays with an ascetic fervour*). 'Into thy hand, O lord, . . . (*Then suddenly, with a look of horror.*) Nothing! To feel one's life blown out like the flame of a cheap match . . .! (*He claps on his mask and laughs harshly.*) To fall asleep and know you'll never, never be called to get on the job of existence again! 'Swift be thine approaching flight! Come soon – soon!' (*He quotes this last with a mocking longing.*)

CYBEL (*pats his head maternally*). There, don't be scared. It's born in the blood. When the time comes, you'll find it's easy.

DION (*jumps to his feet and walks about excitedly*). It won't be long. My wife dragged in a doctor the day before yesterday. He says my heart is gone – booze – He warned me, never another drop or – (*Mockingly.*) What say? Shall we have a drink?

CYBEL (*like an idol*). Suit yourself. It's in the pantry. (*Then, as he hesitates.*) What set you off on this bat? You were raving on about some cathedral plans. . .

DION (*wildly mocking*). They've been accepted – Mr Brown's designs! My designs really! You don't need to be told that. He hands me one mathematically correct barn after another and I doctor them up with cute allurements so that fools will desire to buy, sell, break sleep, love, hate, curse and pray in them! I do this with devilish cleverness to their entire delight! Once I dreamed of painting wind on the sea and the skimming flight of cloud shadows over the tops of trees! Now . . . (*He laughs.*) But pride is a sin – even in a memory of the long deceased! Blessed are the poor in spirit! (*He subsides weakly on his chair, his hand pressed to his heart.*)

CYBEL (*like an idol*). Go home and sleep. Your wife'll be worried.

DION. She knows – but she'll never admit to herself that her husband ever entered your door. (*Mocking.*) Aren't women loyal – to their vanity and their other things!

CYBEL. Brown is coming soon, don't forget.

DION. He knows too and can't admit. Perhaps he needs me here – unknown. What first aroused his passion to possess you exclusively, do you think? Because he knew you loved me and he felt himself cheated. He wanted what he thought was my love of the flesh! He feels I have no right to love. He'd like to steal it as he steals my ideas – complacently – righteously. Oh, the good Brown!

CYBEL. But you like him, too! You're brothers, I guess, somehow.
Well, remember he's paying, he'll pay – in some way or other.

DION (*raises his head as if starting to remove the mask*). I know. Poor
Billy! God forgive me the evil I've done him!

CYBEL (*reaches out and takes his hand*). Poor boy!

DION (*presses her convulsively – then with forced harshness*). Well,
homeward Christian Soldier! I'm off! By-bye, Mother Earth. (*He
starts to go off right. She seems about to let him go.*)

CYBEL (*suddenly starts and calls with deep grief*). Dion! (*He looks at her.
A pause. He comes slowly back. She speaks strangely in a deep, far-off
voice – and yet like a mother talking to her little son.*) You mustn't
forget to kiss me before you go, Dion. (*She removes his mask.*)
Haven't I told you to take off your mask in the house? Look at
me, Dion. I've – just – seen – something. I'm afraid you're
going away a long, long way. I'm afraid I won't see you again for
a long, long time. So it's goodbye, dear. (*She kisses him gently. He
begins to sob. She hands him back his mask.*) Here you are. Don't
get hurt. Remember, it's all a game, and after you're asleep I'll
tuck you in.

DION (*in a choking, heart-broken cry*). Mother! (*Then he claps on his
mask with a terrible effort of will – mockingly.*) Go to the devil, you
sentimental old pig! See you tomorrow! (*He goes, whistling,
slamming the door.*)

CYBEL (*like an idol again*). What's the good of bearing children?
What's the use of giving birth to death? (*She sighs wearily, turns,
puts a plug in the piano, which starts up its old sentimental tune. At
the same moment BROWN enters quietly from the left. He is the ideal of
the still youthful, good-looking, well-groomed, successful provincial
American of forty. Just now, he is plainly perturbed. He is not able to see
either CYBEL's face or her mask.*)

BROWN. Cybel! (*She starts, jams off the music and reaches for her mask,
but has no time to put it on.*) Wasn't that Dion I just saw going out
– after all your promises never to see him! (*She turns like an idol,
holding the mask behind her. He stares, bewildered – stammers.*) I – I
beg your pardon – I thought –

CYBEL (*in her strange voice*). Cybel's gone out to dig in the earth
and pray.

BROWN (*with more assurance*). But – aren't those her clothes?

CYBEL. Cybel doesn't want people to see me naked. I'm her sister.
Dion came to see me.

BROWN (*relieved*). So that's what he's up to, is it? (*Then with a
pitying sigh.*) Poor Margaret! (*Then with playful reproof.*) You

really shouldn't encourage him. He's married and got three big sons.

CYBEL. And you haven't.

BROWN (*stung*). No. I'm not married.

CYBEL. He and I were friends.

BROWN (*with a playful wink*). Yes, I can imagine how the platonic must appeal to Dion's pure innocent type! It's no good kidding me about Dion. We've been friends since we were kids. I know him in and out. I've always stood up for him whatever he's done – so you can be perfectly frank. I only spoke as I did on account of Margaret – his wife – it's pretty tough on her.

CYBEL. You love his wife.

BROWN (*scandalised*). What? What are you talking about? (*Then uncertainly.*) Don't be a fool! (*A pause – then as if impelled by an intense curiosity.*) So Dion is your lover, eh? That's very interesting. (*He pulls his chair closer to hers.*) Sit down. Let's talk. (*She continues to stand, the mask held behind her.*) Tell me – I've always been curious – what is it that makes Dion so attractive to women – especially certain types of women, if you'll pardon me? He always has been and yet I never could see exactly what they saw in him. Is it his looks – or because he's such a violent sensualist – or because he poses as artistic and temperamental – or because he's so wild – or just what is it?

CYBEL. He's alive!

BROWN (*suddenly takes one of her hands and kisses it – insinuatingly*). Well, don't you think I'm alive, too. (*Eagerly.*) Listen. Would you consider giving up Dion – and letting me take care of you under a similar arrangement to the one I've made with Cybel? I like you, you can see that. I won't bother you much – I'm much too busy – you can do what you like – lead your own life – except for seeing him. (*He stops. A pause. She stares ahead unmoved as if she hadn't heard. He pleads.*) Well – what do you say? Please do!

CYBEL (*her voice weary*). Cybel asked me to tell you she'd be back next week, Mr Brown.

BROWN (*with queer agony*). You mean you won't? Don't be so cruel! I love you! (*She walks away. He clutches at her, pleadingly.*) At least – I'll give you anything you ask! – please promise me you won't see Dion Anthony again!

CYBEL (*with deep grief*). He will never see me again, I promise you. Goodbye!

BROWN (*jubilantly, kissing her hand – politely*). Thank you! thank you! I'm exceedingly grateful. (*Tactfully.*) I won't disturb you any further. Please forgive my intrusion, and remember me to Cybel when you write. (*He bows, turns, and goes off left.*)

Curtain.

Scene Two

Scene. The draughting–room in BROWN's *office.* DION's *draughting table with a high stool in front is at centre. Another stool is to the left of it. At the right is a bench. It is in the evening of the same day. The black wall drop has windows painted on it with a dim, street-lighted view of black houses across the way.*

DION *is sitting on the stool behind the table, reading aloud from the 'Imitation of Christ' by Thomas à Kempis to his mask, which is on the table before him. His own face is gentler, more spiritual, more saintlike and ascetic than ever before.*

DION (*like a priest, offering up prayers for the dying*). 'Quickly must thou be gone from hence, see then how matters stand with thee. Ah, fool – learn now to die to the world that thou mayst begin to live with Christ! Do now, beloved, do now all thou canst because thou knowest not when thou shalt die; nor dost thou know what shall befall thee after death. Keep thyself as a pilgrim, and a stranger upon earth, to whom the affairs of this world do not – belong! Keep thy heart free and raised upwards to God because thou hast not here a lasting abode. ' "Because at what hour you know not the Son of Man will come!" ' Amen. (*He raises his hand over the mask as if he were blessing it, closes the book and puts it back in his pocket. He raises the mask in his hands and stares at it with a pitying tenderness.*) Peace, poor tortured one, brave pitiful pride of man, the hour of our deliverance comes. Tomorrow we may be with Him in Paradise! (*He kisses it on the lips and sets it down again. There is the noise of footsteps climbing the stairs in the hallway. He grabs up the mask in a sudden panic and, as a knock comes on the door, he claps it on and calls mockingly.*) Come in, Mrs Anthony, come in!

MARGARET *enters. In one hand behind her, hidden from him, is the mask of the brave face she puts on before the world to hide her suffering and disillusionment, and which she has just taken off. Her own face is still sweet and pretty, but lined, drawn and careworn for its years, sad, resigned, but a bit querulous.*

MARGARET (*wearily reproving*). Thank goodness I've found you! Why haven't you been home the last two days! It's bad enough your drinking again without your staying away and worrying us to death!

DION (*bitterly*). My ears knew her footsteps. One gets to recognise everything – and to see nothing!

MARGARET. I finally sent the boys out looking for you and came myself. (*With tired solicitude.*) I suppose you haven't eaten a thing, as usual. Won't you come home and let me fry you a chop?

DION (*wonderingly*). Can Margaret still love Dion Anthony? Is it possible she does?

MARGARET (*forcing a tired smile*). I suppose so, Dion. I certainly oughtn't to, ought I?

DION (*in same tone*). And I love Margaret! What haunted, haunting ghosts we are! We dimly remember so much it will take us so many million years to forget! (*He comes forward, putting one arm around her bowed shoulders, and they kiss.*)

MARGARET (*patting his hand affectionately*). No, you certainly don't deserve it. When I stop to think of all you've made me go through in the years since we settled down here . . . I really don't believe I could ever have stood it if it weren't for the boys! (*Forcing a smile.*) But perhaps I would, I've always been such a big fool about you.

DION (*a bit mockingly*). The boys! Three strong sons! Margaret can afford to be magnanimous!

MARGARET. If they didn't find you, they were coming to meet me here.

DION (*with sudden wildness – torturedly, sinking on his knees beside her.*) Margaret! Margaret! I'm lonely! I'm frightened! I'm going away! I've got to say goodbye!

MARGARET (*patting his hair*). Poor boy! Poor Dion! Come home and sleep.

DION (*springs up frantically*). No! I'm a man. I'm a lonely man! I can't go back! I have conceived myself! (*Then with desperate mockery.*) Look at me, Mrs Anthony! It's the last chance! Tomorrow I'll have moved on to the next hell! Behold your man – the snivelling, cringing, life-denying Christian slave you have so nobly ignored in the father of your sons! Look! (*He tears the mask from his face, which is radiant with a great pure love for her and a great sympathy and tenderness.*) O woman – my love – that I have sinned against in my sick pride and cruelty – forgive my sins – forgive my solitude – forgive my sickness – forgive me! (*He kneels and kisses the hem of her dress.*)

MARGARET (*who has been staring at him with terror, raising her mask to ward off his face*). Dion! Don't I can't bear it! You're like a ghost. You're dead! Oh my God! Help! Help! (*She falls back fainting on the bench. He looks at her – then takes her hand which holds her mask and looks at that face – gently.*) And now I am permitted to understand and love you, too! (*He kisses the mask first – then kisses her face, murmuring.*) And you, sweetheart! Blessed, thrice blessed are the meek!

There is a sound of heavy, hurrying footsteps on the stairs. He puts on his mask in haste. The three SONS *rush into the room. The* ELDEST *is about fourteen, the two others thirteen and twelve. They look healthy, normal, likeable boys, with much the same quality as* BILLY BROWN*'s in Act One, Scene One. They stop short and stiffen all in a row, staring from the woman on the bench to their father, accusingly.*

ELDEST. We heard some one yell. It sounded like Mother.

DION (*defensively*). No. It was this lady – my wife.

ELDEST. But hasn't Mother come yet?

DION (*going to* MARGARET). Yes. Your Mother is here. (*He stands between them and puts her mask over* MARGARET*'s face – then steps back.*) She has fainted. You'd better bring her to.

BOYS. Mother! (*They run to her side, kneel and rub her wrists. The* ELDEST *smoothes back her hair.*)

DION (*watching them*). At least I am leaving her well provided for. (*He addresses them directly.*) Tell your mother she'll get word from Mr Brown's house. I must pay him a farewell call. I am going Goodbye. (*They stop, staring at him fixedly, with eyes a mixture of bewilderment, distrust and hurt.*)

ELDEST (*awkwardly and shamefacedly*). Honest, I think you ought to have . . .

SECOND. Yes, honest you ought . . .

YOUNGEST. Yes, honest . . .

DION (*in a friendly tone*). I know. But I couldn't. That's for you who can. You must inherit the earth for her. Don't forget now, boys. Goodbye.

BOYS (*in the same awkward, self-conscious tone, one after another*). Goodbye – goodbye – goodbye. (DION *goes.*)

Curtain.

Scene Three

Scene. The library of William BROWN *'s home – night of the same day. A backdrop of carefully painted, prosperous, bourgeois culture, bookcases filled with sets, etc. The heavy table at centre is expensive. The leather arm-chair at left of it and the couch at right are opulently comfortable. The reading lamp on the table is the only light.*

BROWN *sits in the chair at left reading an architectural periodical. His expression is composed and gravely receptive. In outline, his face suggests a Roman consul on an old coin. There is an incongruous distinction about it, the quality of unquestioning faith in the finality of its achievement.*

There is a sudden loud thumping on the front door and the ringing of the bell. BROWN *frowns and listens as a servant answers.* DION *'s voice can be heard, raised mockingly.*

DION. Tell him it's the devil come to conclude a bargain.

BROWN (*suppressing annoyance, calls out with forced good nature*). Come on in, Dion. (DION *enters. He is in a wild state. His clothes are dishevelled, his masked face has a terrible deathlike intensity, its mocking irony becomes so cruelly malignant as to give him the appearance of a real demon, tortured into torturing others.*). Sit down.

DION (*stands and sings*). William Brown's soul lies mouldering in the crib, but his body goes marching on!

BROWN (*maintaining the same indulgent, big-brotherly tone, which he tries to hold throughout the scene.*) Not so loud, for Pete's sake! I don't mind – but I've got neighbours.

DION. Hate them! Fear thy neighbour as thyself! That's the leaden rule for the safe and sane. (*Then advancing to the table with a sort of deadly calm.*) Listen! One day when I was four years old, a boy sneaked up behind when I was drawing a picture in the sand he couldn't draw and hit me on the head with a stick and kicked out my picture and laughed when I cried. It wasn't what he'd done that made me cry, but him! I had loved and trusted him and suddenly the good God was disproved in his person and the devil and injustice of Man was born! Every one called me cry-baby, so I became silent for life and designed a mask of the Bad Boy Pan in which to live and rebel against that other boy's God and protect myself from His cruelty. And that other boy, secretly he felt ashamed but he couldn't acknowledge it; so from that day he instinctively developed into the good boy, the good friend, the good man, William Brown!

BROWN (*shamefacedly*). I remember now. It was a dirty trick. (*Then with a trace of resentment.*) Sit down. You know where the booze is. Have a drink, if you like. But I guess you've had enough already.

DION (*looks at him fixedly for a moment – then strangely*). Thanks be to Brown for reminding me. I must drink. (*He goes and gets a bottle of whisky and a glass.*)

BROWN (*with a good humoured shrug*). All right. It's your funeral.

DION (*returning and pouring out a big drink in the tumbler*). And William Brown's! When I die, he goes to hell! Shoäl! (*He drinks and stares malevolently. In spite of himself,* BROWN *is uneasy. A pause.*)

BROWN (*with forced casualness*). You've been on this toot for a week now.

DION (*tauntingly*). I've been celebrating the acceptance of *my* design for the cathedral.

BROWN (*humorously*). You certainly helped me a lot on it.

DION (*with a harsh laugh*). O perfect Brown! Never mind! I'll make him look in my mirror yet – and drown in it! (*He pours out another big drink.*)

BROWN (*rather tauntingly*). Go easy. I don't want your corpse on my hands.

DION. But I do. (*He drinks.*) Brown will still need me – to reassure him he's alive! I've loved, lusted, won and lost, sung and wept! I've been life's lover! I've fulfilled her will and if she's through with me now it's only because I was too weak to dominate her in turn. It isn't enough to be her creature, you've got to create her or she requests you to destroy yourself.

BROWN (*good naturedly*). Nonsense. Go home and get some sleep.

DION (*as if he hadn't heard – bitingly*). But to be neither creature nor creator! To exist only in her indifference! To be unloved by life! (BROWN *stirs uneasily.*) To be merely a successful freak, the result of some snide neutralizing of life forces – a spineless cactus – a wild boar of the mountains altered into a packer's hog eating to become food – a Don Juan inspired to romance by a monkey's glands – and to have Life not even think you funny enough to see!

BROWN (*stung – angrily*). Bosh!

DION. Consider Mr Brown. His parents bore him on earth as if they were thereby entering him in a baby parade with prizes for the fattest – and he's still being wheeled along in the procession, too fat now to learn to walk, let alone to dance or run, and he'll never live until his liberated dust quickens into earth !

BROWN (*gruffly*). Rave on! (*Then with forced good-nature*). Well,

Dion, at any rate, I'm satisfied.

DION (*quickly and malevolently*). No! Brown isn't satisfied! He's piled on layers of protective fat, but vaguely, deeply he feels at his heart the gnawing of a doubt! And I'm interested in that germ which wriggles like a question mark of insecurity in his blood, because it's part of the creative life Brown's stolen from me!

BROWN (*forcing a sour grin*). Steal germs? I thought you caught them.

DION (*as if he hadn't heard*). It's mine – and I'm interested in seeing it thrive and breed and become multitudes and eat until Brown is consumed!

BROWN (*cannot restrain a shudder*). Sometimes when you're drunk, you're positively evil; do you know it?

DION (*sombrely*). When Pan was forbidden the light and warmth of the sun he grew sensitive and self-conscious and proud and revengeful – and became Prince of Darkness.

BROWN (*jocularly*). You don't fit the rôle of Pan, Dion. It sounds to me like Bacchus, alias the Demon Rum, doing the talking. (DION *recovers from his spasm with a start and stares at* BROWN *with terrible hatred. There is a pause. Inspite of himself,* BROWN *squirms and adopts a placating tone.*) Go home. It's all well enough celebrating our design being accepted, but –

DION (*in a steely voice*). I've been the brains! I've been the design! I've designed even his success – drunk and laughing at him – laughing at his career! Not proud! Sick! Sick of myself and him! Designing and getting drunk? Saving my woman and children! (*He laughs.*) Ha! And this cathedral is my masterpiece! It will make Brown the most eminent architect in this state of God's Country. I put a lot into it – what was left of my life! It's one vivid blasphemy from pavement to the tips of its spires! – but so concealed that the fools will never know. They'll kneel and worship the ironic Silenus who tells them the best good is never to be born! (*He laughs triumphantly.*) Well, blasphemy is faith, isn't it? In self-preservation the devil must believe! But Mr Brown, the Great Brown, has no faith! He couldn't design a cathedral without it looking like the First Supernatural Bank! He only believes in the immortality of the moral belly! (*He laughs wildly – then sinks down in his chair, gasping, his hands pressed to his heart. Then suddenly becomes deadly calm and pronounces like a cruel malignant condemnation.*) From now on, Brown will never design anything. He will devote his life to renovating the house of my Cybel into a home for my Margaret!

BROWN (*springing to his feet, his face convulsed with strange agony*). I've stood enough! How dare you . . .!

DION (*his voice like a probe*). Why has no woman ever loved him? Why has he always been the Big Brother, the Friend? Isn't their trust – a contempt?

BROWN. You lie!

DION. Why has he never been able to love – since my Margaret? Why has he never married? Why has he tried to steal Cybel, as he once tried to steal Margaret? Isn't it out of revenge – and envy?

BROWN (*violently*). Rot! I wanted Cybel, and I bought her!

DION. Brown bought her for me! She has loved me more than he will ever know!

BROWN. You lie! (*Then furiously.*) I'll throw her back on the street!

DION. To me! To her fellow-creature! Why hasn't Brown had children – he who loves children – he who loves *my* children – he who envies me *my* children?

BROWN (*brokenly*). I'm not ashamed to envy you them!

DION. They like Brown, too – as a friend – as an equal – as Margaret has always liked him –

BROWN (*brokenly*). And as I've liked her!

DION. How many million times Brown has thought how much better for her it would have been if she'd chosen him instead!

BROWN (*torturedly*). You lie! (*Then with sudden frenzied defiance.*) All right! If you force me to say it, I do love Margaret! I always have loved her and you've always known I did!

DION (*with a terrible composure*). No! That is merely the appearance, not the truth! Brown loves me! He loves me because I have always possessed the power he needed for love, because I am love!

BROWN (*frenziedly*). You drunken fool! (*He leaps on DION and grabs him by the throat.*)

DION (*triumphantly, staring into his eyes*). Ah! Now he looks into the mirror! Now he sees his face!

BROWN *lets go of him and staggers back to his chair, pale and trembling.*

BROWN (*humbly*). Stop, for God's sake! You're mad!

DION (*sinking in his chair, more and more weakly*). I'm done. My

heart, not Brown – (*Mockingly.*) My last will and testament! I
leave Dion Anthony to William Brown – for him to love and
obey – for him to become me – then my Margaret will love me –
my children will love me – Mr and Mrs Brown and sons, happily
ever after! (*Staggering to his full height and looking upward
defiantly.*) Nothing more – but Man's last gesture – by which he
conquers – to laugh! Ha – (*He begins, stops as if paralysed, and
drops on his knees by* BROWN*'s chair, his mask falling off, his
Christian Martyr's face at the point of death.*) Forgive me, Billy. Bury
me, hide me, forget me for your own happiness! May Margaret
love you! May you design the Temple of Man's Soul! Blessed
are the meek and the poor in spirit! (*He kisses* BROWN*'s feet –
then more and more weakly and childishly.*) What was the prayer,
Billy? I'm getting so sleepy . . .

BROWN (*in a trancelike tone*). 'Our Father who art in Heaven.'

DION (*drowsily*). 'Our Father.' . . .

> *He dies. A pause.* BROWN *remains in a stupor for a moment – then
> stirs himself, puts his hand on* DION*'s breast.*

BROWN (*dully*). He's dead – at last. (*He says this mechanically, but the
last two words awaken him – wonderingly.*) At last? (*Then with
triumph.*) At last! (*He stares at* DION*'s real face contemptuously.*) So
that's the poor weakling you really were! No wonder you hid!
And I've always been afraid of you – yes, I'll confess it now, in
awe of you! Paugh! (*He picks up the mask from the floor.*) No, not
of you! Of this! Say what you like, it's strong if it is bad! And this
is what Margaret loved, not you! Not you! This man! – this man
who willed himself to me! (*Struck by an idea, he jumps to his feet.*)
By God! (*He slowly starts to put the mask on. A knocking comes on the
street door. He starts guiltily, laying the mask on the table. Then he
picks it up again quickly, takes the dead body and carries it off left. He
reappears immediately; and goes to the front door as the knocking
recommences – gruffly.*) Hello! Who's there?

MARGARET. It's Margaret, Billy. I'm looking for Dion.

BROWN (*uncertainly*). Oh – all right – (*Unfastening door.*) Come in.
Hello, Margaret. Hello, Boys! He's here. He's asleep. I – I was
just dozing off too.

> MARGARET *enters. She is wearing her mask. The three* SONS *are
> with her.*

MARGARET (*seeing the bottle, forcing a laugh*). Has he been
celebrating?

BROWN (*with strange glibness now*). No. I was. He wasn't. He said
he'd sworn off tonight – for ever – for your sake – and the kids!

MARGARET (*with amazed joy*). Dion said that? (*Then hastily defensive.*) But of course he never does drink much. Where is he?

BROWN. Upstairs. I'll wake him. He felt bad. He took off his clothes to take a bath before he lay down. You just wait here.

She sits in the chair where DION *had sat and stares straight before her. The* SONS *group around her, as if for a family photo.* BROWN *hurries out left.*

MARGARET. It's late to keep you boys up. Aren't you sleepy?

BOYS. No, Mother.

MARGARET (*proudly*). I'm glad to have three such strong boys to protect me.

ELDEST (*boastingly*). We'd kill anyone that touched you, wouldn't we?

NEXT. You bet! We'd make him wish he hadn't!

YOUNGEST. You bet!

MARGARET. You're Mother's brave boys! (*She laughs fondly – then curiously.*) Do you like Mr Brown?

ELDEST. Sure thing! He's a regular fellow.

NEXT. He's all right!

YOUNGEST. Sure thing!

MARGARET (*half to herself*). Your father claims he steals his ideas.

ELDEST (*with a sheepish grin*). I'll bet father said that when he was – just talking.

NEXT. Mr Brown doesn't have to steal, does he?

YOUNGEST. I should say not! He's awful rich.

MARGARET. Do you love your father?

ELDEST (*scuffling – embarrassed*). Why – of course –

NEXT (*ditto*). Sure thing!

YOUNGEST. Sure I do.

MARGARET (*with a sigh*). I think you'd better start on before – right now – before your father comes – He'll be very sick and nervous and he'll want to be quiet. So run along!

BOYS. All right.

They file out and close the front door as BROWN, *dressed in* DION'*s clothes and wearing his mask, appears at left.*

MARGARET (*taking off her mask, gladly*). Dion! (*She stares wonderingly at him and he at her; goes to him and puts an arm around him.*) Poor dear, do you feel sick? (*He nods.*) But you look – (*Squeezing his arms.*) – why, you actually feel stronger and better already! Is it true what Billy told me – about your swearing off for ever? (*He nods. She exclaims intensely.*) Oh, if you'll only – and get well – we can still be so happy! Give Mother a kiss. (*They kiss. A shudder passes through both of them. She breaks away laughing with aroused desire.*) Why, Dion? Aren't you ashamed? You haven't kissed me like that for ages!

BROWN (*his voice imitating* DION*'s and muffled by the mask*). I've wanted to, Margaret!

MARGARET (*gaily and coquettishly now*). Were you afraid I'd spurn you? Why, Dion, something has happened. It's like a miracle! Even your voice is changed? It actually sounds younger; do you know it? (*Then, solicitously.*) But you must be worn out. Let's go home. (*With an impulsive movement she flings her arms wide open, throwing her mask away from her as if suddenly no longer needing it.*) Oh, I'm beginning to feel so happy, Dion – so happy!

BROWN (*stifledly*). Let's go home. (*She puts her arm around him. They walk to the door.*)

Curtain.

ACT THREE

Scene One

Scene. The draughting-room and private office of BROWN *are both shown. The former is on the left, the latter on the right of a dividing wall at the centre. The arrangement of furniture in each room is the same as in previous scenes. It is ten in the morning of a day about a month later. The backdrop for both rooms is of plain wall with a few tacked-up designs and blue prints painted on it.*

Two DRAUGHTSMEN, *a middle-aged man and a young man, both stoop-shouldered, are sitting on stools behind what was formerly* DION's *table. They are tracing plans. They talk as they work.*

OLDER DRAUGHTSMAN. W. B. is late again.

YOUNGER DRAUGHTSMAN. Wonder what's got into him the last month? (*A pause. They work silently.*)

OLDER DRAUGHTSMAN. Yes, ever since he fired Dion . . .

YOUNGER DRAUGHTSMAN. Funny his firing him all of a sudden like that. (*A pause. They work.*)

OLDER DRAUGHTSMAN. I haven't seen Dion around town since then. Have you?

YOUNGER DRAUGHTSMAN. No, not since Brown told us he'd sacked him. I suppose he's off drowning his sorrow!

OLDER DRAUGHTSMAN. I heard some one had seen him at home and he was sober and looking fine. (*A pause. They work.*)

YOUNGER DRAUGHTSMAN. What got into Brown? They say he fired all his old servants that same day and only uses his house to sleep in.

OLDER DRAUGHTSMAN (*with a sneer*). Artistic temperament, maybe – the real name of which is swelled head! (*There is a noise of footsteps from the hall. Warningly.*) Ssstt!

They bend over their table. MARGARET *enters. She does not need to wear a mask now. Her face has regained the self-confident spirit of its youth, her eyes shine with happiness.*

MARGARET (*heartily*). Good morning! What a lovely day!

BOTH (*perfunctorily*). Good morning, Mrs Anthony .

MARGARET (*looking around*). You've been changing around in here, haven't you? Where is Dion? (*They stare at her.*) I forgot to tell him something important this morning and our phone's out of order. So if you'll tell him I'm here – (*They don't move. A pause.* MARGARET *says stiffly.*) Oh, I realise Mr Brown has given strict orders Dion is not to be disturbed, but surely . . . (*Sharply.*) Where is my husband, please?

OLDER DRAUGHTSMAN. We don't know.

MARGARET. You don't know?

YOUNGER DRAUGHTSMAN. We haven't seen him.

MARGARET. Why, he left home at eight-thirty!

OLDER DRAUGHTSMAN. To come here?

YOUNGER DRAUGHTSMAN. This morning?

MARGARET (*provoked*). Why, of course, to come here – as he does every day! (*They stare at her. A pause.*)

OLDER DRAUGHTSMAN (*evasively*). We haven't seen him.

MARGARET (*with asperity*). Where is Mr Brown?

YOUNGER DRAUGHTSMAN (*at a noise of footsteps from the hall – sulkily*). Coming now.

BROWN *enters. He is now wearing a mask which is an exact likeness of his face as it was in the last scene – the self-assured success. When he sees* MARGARET, *he starts back apprehensively.*

BROWN (*immediately controlling himself – breezily*). Hello, Margaret! This is a pleasant surprise! (*He holds out his hand.*)

MARGARET (*hardly taking it – reservedly*). Good morning.

BROWN (*turning quickly to the* DRAUGHTSMEN). I hope you explained to Mrs Anthony how busy Dion . . .

MARGARET (*interrupting him – stiffly*). I certainly can't understand –

BROWN (*hastily*). I'll explain. Come in here and be comfortable. (*He throws open the door and ushers her into his private office.*)

OLDER DRAUGHTSMAN. Dion must be putting over some bluff on her.

YOUNGER DRAUGHTSMAN. Pretending he's still here – and Brown's helping him . . .

OLDER DRAUGHTSMAN. But why should Brown, after he . . .?

YOUNGER DRAUGHTSMAN. Well, I suppose – Search me. (*They work.*)

BROWN. Have a chair, Margaret. (*She sits on the chair stiffly. He sits behind the desk.*)

MARGARET (*coldly*). I'd like some explanation . . .

BROWN (*coaxingly*). Now, don't get angry, Margaret! Dion is hard at work on his design for the new State Capitol, and I don't want him disturbed, not even by you! So be a good sport! It's for his own good, remember! I asked him to explain to you.

MARGARET (*relenting*). He told me you'd agreed to ask me and the boys not to come here – but then, we hardly ever did.

BROWN. But you might! (*Then with confidential friendliness.*) This is for his sake, Margaret. I know Dion. He's got to be able to work without distractions. He's not the ordinary man; you appreciate that. And this design means his whole future! He's to get full credit for it, and as soon as it's accepted, I take him into partnership. It's all agreed. And after that I'm going to take a long vacation – go to Europe for a couple of years – and leave everything here in Dion's hands! Hasn't he told you all this?

MARGARET (*jubilant now*). Yes – but I could hardly believe . . . (*Proudly.*) I'm sure he can do it. He's been like a new man lately, so full of ambition and energy! It's made me so happy! (*She stops in confusion.*)

BROWN (*deeply moved, takes her hand impulsively*). And it has made me happy, too!

MARGARET (*confused – with an amused laugh*). Why, Billy Brown! For a moment, I thought it was Dion, your voice sounded so much . . . !

BROWN (*with sudden desperation*). Margaret, I've got to tell you! I can't go on like this any longer! I've got to confess . . . ! There's something . . .!

MARGARET (*alarmed*). Not – not about Dion?

BROWN (*harshly*). To hell with Dion! To hell with Billy Brown! (*He tears off his mask and reveals a suffering face that is ravaged and haggard, his own face tortured and distorted by the demon of DION's mask.*) Think of me! I love you, Margaret! Leave him! I've always loved you! Come away with me! I'll sell out here! We'll go abroad and be happy!

MARGARET (*amazed*). Billy Brown, do you realise what you're saying? (*With a shudder.*) Are you crazy? Your face – is terrible. You're sick! Shall I phone for a doctor?

BROWN (*turning away slowly and putting on his mask – dully*). No. I've been on the verge – of a breakdown – for sometime. I get spells . . . I'm better now. (*He turns back to her.*) Forgive me! Forget what I said! But, for all our sakes, don't come here again.

MARGARET (*coldly*). After this – I assure you . . . ! (*Then looking at him with pained incredulity.*) Why, Billy – I simply won't believe – after all these years . . . !

BROWN. It will never happen again. Goodbye.

MARGARET. Goodbye. (*Then, wishing to leave on a pleasant change of subject – forcing a smile.*) Don't work Dion to death! He's never home for dinner any more.

She goes out past the DRAUGHTSMEN *and off right, rear.* BROWN *sits down at his desk, taking off the mask again. He stares at it with bitter, cynical amusement.*

BROWN. You're dead, William Brown, dead beyond hope of resurrection! It's the Dion you buried in your garden who killed you, not you him! It's Margaret's husband who . . . (*He laughs harshly.*) Paradise by proxy! Love by mistaken identity! God! (*This is almost a prayer – then fiercely defiant.*) But it is paradise! I *do* love!

As he is speaking, a well-dressed, important, stout man enters the draughting-room. He is carrying a rolled-up plan in his hand. He nods condescendingly and goes directly to BROWN*'s door, on which he raps sharply, and, without waiting for an answer, turns the knob.* BROWN *has just time to turn his head and get his mask on.*

MAN (*briskly*). Ah, good morning! I came right in. Hope I didn't disturb . . . ?

BROWN (*the successful architect now – urbanely*). Not at all, sir. How are you? (*They shake hands.*) Sit down. Have a cigar. And now what can I do for you this morning?

MAN (*unrolling his plan*). It's your plan. My wife and I have been going over it again. We like it – and we don't – and when a man plans to lay out half a million, why he wants everything exactly right, eh? (BROWN *nods.*) It's too cold, too spare, too like a tomb, if you'll pardon me, for a liveable home. Can't you liven it up, put in some decorations, make it fancier and warmer – you know what I mean. (*Looks at him a bit doubtfully.*) People tell me you had an assistant, Anthony, who was a real shark on these details but that you've fired him –

BROWN (*suavely*). Gossip! He's still with me but, for reasons of his own, doesn't wish it known. Yes, I trained him and he's very

ingenious. I'll turn this right over to him and instruct him to
carry out your wishes.

Curtain.

Scene Two

Scene. The same as Act Two, Scene Three – the library of BROWN'*s home
about eight the same night. He can be heard feeling his way in through the
dark. He switches on the reading lamp on the table. Directly under it on a
sort of stand is the mask of* DION, *its empty eyes staring front.*

BROWN *takes off his own mask and lays it on the table before* DION'*s. He
flings himself down in the chair and stares without moving into the eyes of*
DION'*s mask. Finally, he begins to talk to it in a bitter, mocking tone.*

BROWN. Listen! Today was a narrow escape – for us! We can't
avoid discovery much longer. We must get our plot to working!
We've already made William Brown's will, leaving you his
money and business. We must hustle off to Europe now – and
murder him there! (*A bit tauntingly.*) Then you – the I in you – *I*
will live with Margaret happily ever after. (*More tauntingly.*) She
will have children by me! (*He seems to hear some mocking denial
from the mask. He bends toward it.*) What? (*Then with a sneer.*)
Anyway, that doesn't matter! Your children already love me
more than they ever loved you! And Margaret loves me more!
You think you've won, do you – that I've got to vanish into you
in order to live? Not yet my friend! Never! Wait! Gradually
Margaret will love what is beneath – me! Little by little I'll teach
her to know me, and then finally I'll reveal myself to her, and
confess that I stole your place out of love for her, and she'll
understand and forgive and love me! And you'll be forgotten!
Ha! (*Again he bends down to the mask as if listening – torturedly.*)
What's that? She'll never believe? She'll never see? She'll never
understand? You lie, devil! (*He reaches out his hands as if to take
the mask by the throat, then shrinks back with a shudder of hopeless
despair.*) God have mercy! Let me believe! Blessed are the
merciful! Let me obtain mercy! (*He waits, his face upturned –
pleadingly.*) Not yet? (*Despairingly.*) Never? (*A pause. Then, in a
sudden panic of dread, he reaches out for the mask of* DION *like a dope
fiend after a drug. As soon as he holds it, he seems to gain strength and
is able to force a sad laugh.*) Now I am drinking your strength,
Dion – strength to love in this world and die and sleep and
become fertile earth, as you are becoming now in my garden –
your weakness the strength of my flowers, your failure as an
artist painting their petals with life! (*Then, with bravado.*) Come
with me while Margaret's bridegroom dresses in your clothes,

Mr Anthony! I need the devil when I'm in the dark! (*He goes off left, but can be heard talking.*) Your clothes begin to fit me better than my own! Hurry, Brother! It's time we were home. Our wife is waiting! (*He reappears, having changed his coat and trousers.*) Come with me and tell her again I love her! Come and hear her tell me how she loves you! (*He suddenly cannot help kissing the mask.*) I love you because she loves you! My kisses on your lips are for her! (*He puts the mask over his face and stands for a moment, seeming to grow tall and proud – then with a laugh of bold self-assurance.*) Out by the back way! I mustn't forget I'm a desperate criminal, pursued by God, and by myself! (*He goes out right, laughing with amused satisfaction.*)

Curtain.

Scene Three

Is the same as Scene One of Act One – the sitting-room of MARGARET*'s home. It is about half an hour after the last scene.* MARGARET *sits on the sofa, waiting with the anxious, impatient expectancy of one deeply in love. She is dressed with a careful, subtle extra touch to attract the eye. She looks young and happy. She is trying to read a book. The front door is heard opening and closing. She leaps up and runs back to throw her arms around* BROWN *as he enters from right, rear. She kisses him passionately.*

MARGARET (*as he recoils with a sort of guilt – laughingly*). Why, you hateful old thing, you! I really believe you were trying to avoid kissing me! Well, just for that, I'll never . . .

BROWN (*with fierce, defiant passion, kisses her again and again*). Margaret!

MARGARET. Call me Peggy again. You used to when you really loved me. (*Softly.*) Remember the school commencement dance – you and I on the dock in the moonlight?

BROWN (*with pain*). No. (*He takes his arms from around her.*)

MARGARET (*still holding him – with a laugh*). Well, I like that! You old bear, you! Why not?

BROWN (*sadly*). It was so long ago.

MARGARET (*a bit melancholy*). You mean you don't want to be reminded that we're getting old?

BROWN. Yes. (*He kisses her gently.*) I'm tired. Let's sit down. (*They sit on the sofa, his arm about her, her head on his shoulder.*)

MARGARET (*with a happy sigh*). I don't mind remembering – now

I'm happy. It's only when I'm unhappy that it hurts – and I've been so happy lately, dear – and so grateful to you! (*He stirs uneasily. She goes on joyfully.*) Everything's changed! I'd got pretty resigned to – and sad and hopeless, too – and then all at once you turn right around and everything is the same as when we were first married – much better even, for I was never sure of you then. You were always so strange and aloof and alone, it seemed I was never really touching you. But now I feel you've become quite human – like me – and I'm so happy, dear! (*She kisses him.*)

BROWN (*his voice trembling*). Then I have made you happy – happier than ever before – no matter what happens? (*She nods.*) Then – that justifies everything! (*He forces a laugh.*)

MARGARET. Of course it does! I've always known that. But you – you wouldn't be – or you couldn't be – and I could never help you – and all the time I knew you were so lonely! I could always hear you calling to me that you were lost, but I couldn't find the path to you because I was lost, too! That's an awful way for a wife to feel! (*She laughs – joyfully.*) But now you're here! You're mine! You're my long-lost lover, and my husband, and my big boy, too!

BROWN (*with a trace of jealousy*). Where are your other big boys tonight?

MARGARET. Out to a dance. They've all acquired girls, I'll have you know.

BROWN (*mockingly*). Aren't you jealous?

MARGARET (*gaily*). Of course! Terribly! But I'm diplomatic. I don't let them see. (*Changing the subject.*) Believe me, they've noticed the change in you! The eldest was saying to me today: 'It's great not to have Father so nervous, any more. Why, he's a regular sport when he gets started!' And the other two said very solemnly: 'You bet!' (*She laughs.*)

BROWN (*brokenly*). I – I'm glad.

MARGARET. Dion! You're crying!

BROWN (*stung by the name, gets up – harshly*). Nonsense! Did you ever know Dion to cry about anyone?

MARGARET (*sadly*). You couldn't – then. You were too lonely. You had no one to cry to.

BROWN (*goes and takes a rolled-up plan from the table drawer – dully*). I've got to do some work.

MARGARET (*disappointedly*). What, has that old Billy Brown got you to work at home again, too?

BROWN (*ironically*). It's for Dion's good, you know – and yours.

MARGARET (*making the best of it – cheerfully*). All right, I won't be
selfish. It really makes me proud for you to be so ambitious. Let
me help.

*She brings his drawing-board, which he puts on the table and pins his
plan upon. She sits on sofa and picks up her book.*

BROWN (*carefully casual*). I hear you were in to see me today?

MARGARET. Yes, and Billy wouldn't hear of it! I was quite furious
until he convinced me it was all for the best. When is he going
to take you into partnership?

BROWN. Very soon now.

MARGARET. And will he really give you full charge when he goes
abroad?

BROWN. Yes.

MARGARET (*practically*). I'd pin him down if I could. Promises are
all right, but – (*She hesitates.*) I don't trust him.

BROWN (*with a start, sharply*). What makes you say that?

MARGARET. Oh, something that happened today.

BROWN. What?

MARGARET. I don't mean I blame him, but – to be frank, I think
the Great God Brown, as you call him, is getting a bit queer and
it's time he took a vacation. Don't you?

BROWN (*his voice a bit excited – but guardedly*). But why? What did he
do?

MARGARET (*hesitatingly*). Well – it's really too silly – he suddenly
got awfully strange. His face scared me. It was like a corpse.
Then he raved on some nonsense about he'd always loved me.
He went on like a perfect fool! (*She looks at BROWN, who is
staring at her. She becomes uneasy.*) Maybe I shouldn't tell you this.
He simply wasn't responsible. Then he came to himself and was
all right and begged my pardon and seemed dreadfully sorry,
and I felt sorry for him. (*Then with a shudder.*) But honestly,
Dion, it was just too disgusting for words to hear him! (*With
kind, devastating contempt.*) Poor Billy!

BROWN (*with a show of tortured derision*). Poor Billy! Poor Billy the
Goat! (*With mocking frenzy.*) I'll kill him for you! I'll serve you his
heart for breakfast!

MARGARET (*jumping up – frightenedly*). Dion!

BROWN (*waving his pencil knife with grotesque flourishes*). I tell you I'll murder this God-damned disgusting Great God Brown who stands like a fatted calf in the way of our health and wealth and happiness!

MARGARET (*bewilderedly, not knowing how much is pretending, puts an arm about him*). Don't, dear! You're being horrid and strange again. It makes me afraid you haven't really changed, after all.

BROWN (*unheeding*). And then my wife can be happy! Ha! (*He laughs. She begins to cry. He controls himself – pats her head – gently.*) All right, dear. Mr Brown is now safely in hell. Forget him!

MARGARET (*stops crying – but still worriedly*). I should never have told you – but I never imagined you'd take it seriously. I've never thought of Billy Brown except as a friend, and lately not even that! He's just a stupid old fool!

BROWN. Ha–ha! Didn't I say he was in hell? They're torturing him! (*Then controlling himself again – exhaustedly*). Please leave me alone now. I've got to work.

MARGARET. All right dear. I'll go into the next room and anything you want, just call. (*She pats his face – cajolingly.*) Is it all forgotten?

BROWN. Will you be happy?

MARGARET. Yes.

BROWN. Then it's dead, I promise! (*She kisses him and goes out. He stares ahead, then shakes off his thoughts and concentrates on his work – mockingly.*) Our beautiful new Capitol calls you, Mr Dion! To work! We'll adroitly hide old Silenus on the cupola! Let him dance over their law-making with his eternal leer! (*He bends over his work.*)

Curtain.

ACT FOUR

Scene One

Scene. Same as Scene One of Act Three – the draughting-room and
BROWN*'s office. It is dusk of a day about a month later.*

The two draughtsmen are bent over their table, working.

BROWN, *at his desk, is working feverishly over a plan. He is wearing the*
mask of DION. *The mask of* WILLIAM BROWN *rests on the desk beside*
him. As he works, he chuckles with malicious glee – finally flings down his
pencil with a flourish.

BROWN. Done! In the name of the Almighty Brown, amen, amen!
    Here's a wondrous fair capitol! The design would do just as well
    for a Home for Criminal Imbeciles! Yet to them, such is my art,
    it will appear to possess a pure commonsense, a fat-bellied
    finality, as dignified as the suspenders of an assemblyman! Only
    to me will that pompous façade reveal itself as the wearily ironic
    grin of Pan as, his ears drowsy with the crumbling hum of past
    and future civilisations, he half-listens to the laws passed by his
    fleas to enslave him! Ha–ha–ha! (*He leaps grotesquely from behind*
    his desk and cuts a few goatish capers, laughing with lustful
    merriment.) Long live Chief of Police Brown! District Attorney
    Brown! Alderman Brown! Assemblyman Brown! Mayor Brown!
    Congressman Brown! Governor Brown! Senator Brown!
    President Brown! (*He chants.*) Oh, how many persons in one
    God make up the good God Brown? Hahahaha! (*The two*
    DRAUGHTSMEN *in the next room have stopped work and are*
    listening.)

YOUNGER DRAUGHTSMAN. Drunk as a fool!

OLDER DRAUGHTSMAN. At least Dion used to have the decency
    to stay away from the office –

YOUNGER DRAUGHTSMAN. Funny how it's got hold of Brown so
    quick!

OLDER DRAUGHTSMAN. He was probably hitting it up on the
    Q.T. all the time.

BROWN (*has come back to his desk, laughing to himself and out of*
    breath). Time to become respectable again! (*He takes off the*
    DION *mask and reaches out for the* WILLIAM BROWN *one – then*

stops, with a hand on each, staring down on the plan with fascinated loathing. His real face is now sick, ghastly, tortured hollow-cheeked and feverish-eyed.) Ugly! Hideous! Despicable! Why must the demon in me pander to cheapness – then punish me with self-loathing and life-hatred? Why am I not strong enough to perish – or blind enough to be content? (*To heaven, bitterly but pleadingly.*) Give me the strength to destroy this! — and myself – and him! — and I will believe in Thee! (*While he has been speaking there has been a noise from the stairs. The two* DRAUGHTSMEN *have bent over their work.* MARGARET *enters, closing the door behind her. At this sound,* BROWN *starts. He immediately senses who it is – with alarm.*) Margaret! (*He grabs up both masks and goes into room off right.*)

MARGARET (*She looks healthy and happy, but her face wears a worried, solicitous expression – pleasantly to the staring* DRAUGHTSMEN). Good morning. Oh, you needn't look worried, it's Mr Brown I want to see, not my husband.

YOUNGER DRAUGHTSMAN (*hesitatingly*). He's locked himself in – but maybe if you'll knock –

MARGARET (*knocks – somewhat embarrassedly*). Mr Brown!

BROWN *enters his office, wearing the* WILLIAM BROWN *mask. He comes quickly to the other door and unlocks it.*

BROWN (*with a hectic cordiality*). Come on, Margaret! Enter! This is delightful! Sit down! What can I do for you?

MARGARET (*taken aback – a bit stiffly*). Nothing much.

BROWN. Something about Dion, of course. Well, your darling pet is all right – never better!

MARGARET (*coldly*). That's a matter of opinion. I think you're working him to death.

BROWN. Oh, no, not him. It's Brown who is to die. We've agreed on that.

MARGARET (*giving him a queer look*). I'm serious.

BROWN. So am I. Deadly serious! Hahaha!

MARGARET (*checking her indignation*). That's what I came to see you about. Really, Dion has acted so hectic and on edge lately I'm sure he's on the verge of a breakdown.

BROWN. Well, it certainly isn't drink. He hasn't had a drop. He doesn't need it! Haha! And I haven't either, although the gossips are beginning to say I'm soused all the time! It's because I've started to laugh! Hahaha! They can't believe in joy in this town except by the bottle! What funny little people!

Hahaha! When you're the Great God Brown, eh, Margaret?
Hahaha!

MARGARET (*getting up – uneasily*). I'm afraid I –

BROWN. Don't be afraid, my dear! I won't make love to you again!
Honour bright! I'm too near the grave for such folly! But it
must have been funny for you when you came here the last time
– watching a disgusting old fool like me, eh? – too funny for
words! Hahaha! (*Then with a sudden movement he flourishes the
design before her.*) Look! We've finished it! Dion has finished it!
His fame is made!

MARGARET (*tartly*). Really, Billy, I believe you are drunk!

BROWN. Nobody kisses me – so you can all believe the worst!
Hahaha!

MARGARET (*chillingly*). Then if Dion is through, why can't I see
him?

BROWN (*crazily*). See Dion? See Dion? Well, why not? It's an age of
miracles. The streets are full of Lazaruses. Pray! I mean – wait a
moment, if you please.

BROWN *disappears into the room off right. A moment later he reappears
in the mask of* DION. *He holds out his arms and* MARGARET *rushes
into them. They kiss passionately. Finally he sits with her on the lounge.*

MARGARET. So you've finished it.

BROWN. Yes. The Committee is coming to see it soon. I've made
all the changes they'll like, the fools!

MARGARET (*lovingly*). And can we go on that second honeymoon,
right away now?

BROWN. In a week or so, I hope – as soon as I've got Brown off to
Europe.

MARGARET. Tell me – isn't he drinking hard?

BROWN (*laughing as* BROWN *did*). Haha! Soused to the ears all
the time! Soused on life! He can't stand it! It's burning his
insides out!

MARGARET (*alarmed*). Dear! I'm worried about you. You sound as
crazy as he did – when you laugh! You must rest!

BROWN (*controlling himself*). I'll rest in peace – when he's gone!

MARGARET (*with a queer look*). Why, Dion, that isn't your suit. It's
just like –

BROWN. It's his! We're getting to be like twins! I'm inheriting his
clothes already! (*Then calming himself as he sees how frightened she*

is.) Don't be worried, dear. I'm just a trifle elated, now the job's done. I guess I'm a bit soused on life, too!

The COMMITTEE, *three important-looking, average personages, come into the draughting-room.*

MARGARET (*forcing a smile.*) Well, don't let it burn *your* insides out!

BROWN. No danger! Mine were tempered in hell! Hahaha!

MARGARET (*kissing him, coaxingly*). Come home, dear – please!

OLDER DRAUGHTSMAN (*knocks on the door*). The Committee is here, Mr Brown.

BROWN (*hurriedly to* MARGARET). You receive them. Hand them the design. I'll get Brown. (*He raises his voice.*) Come right in, gentlemen.

He goes off right, as the COMMITTEE *enter the office. When they see* MARGARET, *they stop in surprise.*

MARGARET (*embarrassedly*). Good afternoon. Mr Brown will be right with you. (*They bow.* MARGARET *holds out the design to them.*) This is my husband's design. He finished it today.

COMMITTEE. Ah! (*They crowd around to look at it – with enthusiasm.*) Perfect! Splendid! Couldn't be better! Exactly what we suggested.

MARGARET (*joyfully*). Then you accept it? Mr Anthony will be so pleased!

MEMBER. Mr Anthony?

ANOTHER. Is he working here again?

THIRD. Did I understand you to say this was your husband's design?

MARGARET (*excitedly*). Yes! Entirely his! He's worked like a dog – (*Appalled.*) You don't mean to say – Mr Brown never told you? (*They shake their heads in solemn surprise.*) Oh, the contemptible cad! I hate him!

BROWN (*appearing at right – mockingly*). Hate me, Margaret? Hate Brown? How superfluous! (*Oratorically.*) Gentlemen, I have been keeping a secret from you in order that you might be the more impressed when I revealed it. That design is entirely the inspiration of Mr Dion Anthony's genius. I had nothing to do with it.

MARGARET (*contritely*). Oh, Billy! I'm sorry! Forgive me!

BROWN (*ignoring her, takes the plan from the* COMMITTEE *and begins unpinning it from the board – mockingly*). I can see by your faces you have approved this. You are delighted, aren't you? And why not, my dear sirs? Look at it, and look at you! Hahaha!

It'll immortalise you, my good men! You'll be as death-defying a joke as any in Joe Miller! (*Then with a sudden complete change of tone – angrily.*) You damn fools! Can't you see this is an insult – a terrible, blasphemous insult! – that this embittered failure Anthony is hurling in the teeth of our success – an insult to you, to me, to you, Margaret – and to Almighty God! (*In a frenzy of fury.*) And if you are weak and cowardly enough to stand for it, I'm not!

He tears the plan into four pieces. The COMMITTEE *stand aghast.* MARGARET *runs forward.*

MARGARET (*in a scream*). You coward! Dion! Dion! (*She picks up the plan and hugs it to her bosom.*)

BROWN (*with a sudden goatish caper*). I'll tell him you're here. (*He disappears, but reappears almost immediately in the mask of* DION. *He is imposing a terrible discipline on himself to avoid dancing and laughing. He speaks suavely.*) Everything is all right – all for the best – you mustn't get excited! A little paste, Margaret! A little paste, gentlemen! And all will be well. Life is imperfect, Brothers! Men have their faults, Sister! But with a few drops of glue much may be done! A little dab of pasty resignation here and there – and even broken hearts may be repaired to do yeoman service! (*He has edged toward the door. They are all staring at him with petrified bewilderment. He puts his finger to his lips.*) Sssh! This is Daddy's bedtime secret for today: Man is born broken. He lives by mending. The grace of God is glue! (*With a quick prancing movement, he has opened the door, gone through, and closed it after him silently, shaking with suppressed laughter. He springs lightly to the side of the petrified* DRAUGHTSMEN *– in a whisper.*) They will find him in the little room. Mr William Brown is dead!

With light leaps he vanishes, his head thrown back, shaking with silent laughter. The sound of his feet leaping down the stairs, five at a time, can be heard. Then a pause of silence. The people in the two rooms stare. The YOUNGER DRAUGHTSMAN *is the first to recover.*

YOUNGER DRAUGHTSMAN (*rushing into the next room, shouts in terrified tones*). Mr Brown is dead!

COMMITTEE. He murdered him!

They all run into the little room off right. MARGARET *remains, stunned with horror. They return in a moment, carrying the mask of* WILLIAM BROWN, *two on each side, as if they were carrying a body by the legs and shoulders. They solemnly lay him down on the couch and stand looking down at him.*

FIRST COMMITTEEMAN (*with a frightened awe*). I can't believe he's gone.

SECOND COMMITTEEMAN (*in same tone*). I can almost hear him talking. (*As if impelled, he clears his throat and addresses the mask importantly.*) Mr Brown – (*Then stops short.*)

THIRD COMMITTEEMAN (*shrinking back*). No. Dead, all right! (*Then suddenly, hysterically angry and terrified.*) We must take steps at once to run Anthony to earth!

MARGARET (*with a heart-broken cry*). Dion's innocent!

YOUNGER DRAUGHTSMAN. I'll phone for the police, sir! (*He rushes to the phone.*)

Curtain.

Scene Two

Scene. The same as Scene Two of Act Three – the library of WILLIAM BROWN*'s home. The mask of* DION *stands on the table beneath the light, facing front.*

On his knees beside the table, facing front, stripped naked except for a while cloth around his loins, is BROWN. *The clothes he has torn off in his agony are scattered on the floor. His eyes, his arms, his whole body strain upward, his muscles writhe with his lips as they pray silently in their agonised supplication. Finally a voice seems torn out of him.*

BROWN. Mercy, Compassionate Saviour of Man! Out of my depths I cry to you! Mercy on thy poor clod, thy clot of unhallowed earth, thy clay, the Great God Brown! Mercy, Saviour! (*He seems to wait for an answer – then leaping to his feet he puts out one hand to touch the mask like a frightened child reaching out for its nurse's hand – then with immediate mocking despair.*) Bah! I am sorry, little children, but your kingdom is empty. God has become disgusted and moved away to some far ecstatic star where life is a dancing flame! We must die without him. (*Then – addressing the mask – harshly.*) Together, my friend! You, too! Let Margaret suffer! Let the whole world suffer as I am suffering!

There is a sound of a door being pushed violently open, padding feet in slippers, and CYBEL, *wearing her mask, runs into the room. She stops short on seeing* BROWN *and the mask, and stares from one to the other for a second in confusion. She is dressed in a black kimono robe and wears slippers over her bare feet. Her yellow hair hangs down in a great mane over her shoulders. She has grown stouter, has more of the deep objective calm of an idol.*

BROWN (*staring at her – fascinated – with great peace as if her presence comforted him*). Cybel! I was coming to you! How did you know?

CYBEL (*takes off her mask and looks from Brown to the* DION *mask, now with a great understanding*). So that's why you never came to me again! You are Dion Brown!

BROWN (*bitterly*). I am the remains of William Brown! (*He points out to the mask of* DION.) I am his murderer and his murdered!

CYBEL (*with a laugh of exasperated pity*). Oh, why can't you ever learn to leave yourselves alone and leave me alone.

BROWN (*boyishly and naïvely*). I am Billy.

CYBEL (*immediately, with a motherly solicitude*). Then run, Billy, run! They are hunting for some one! They came to my place, hunting for a murderer, Dion! They must find a victim! They've got to quiet their fears, to cast our their devils, or they'll never sleep soundly again! They've got to absolve themselves by finding a guilty one! They've got to kill some one now, to live! You're naked! You must be Satan! Run, Billy, run! They'll come here! I ran here to warn – some one! So run away if you want to live!

BROWN (*like a sulky child*). I'm too tired. I don't want to.

CYBEL (*with motherly calm*). All right, you needn't, Billy. Don't sulk. (*As a noise comes from outside.*) Anyway, it's too late. I hear them in the garden now.

BROWN (*listening, puts out his hand and takes the mask of* DION – *as he gains strength, mockingly*). Thanks for this one last favour, Dion! Listen! Your avengers! Standing on your grave in the garden! Hahaha! (*He puts on the mask and springs to the left and makes a gesture as if flinging French windows open. Gaily mocking.*) Welcome, dumb worshippers! I am your Great God Brown! I have been advised to run from you but it is my almighty whim to dance into escape over your prostrate souls!

Shouts from the garden and a volley of shots. BROWN *staggers back and falls on the floor by the couch, mortally wounded.*

CYBEL (*runs to his side, lifts him on to the couch and takes of the mask of* DION). You can't take this to bed with you. You've got to sleep alone.

She places the mask of DION *back on its stand under the light and puts on her own, just as, after a banging of doors, crashing of glass, trampling of feet, a* SQUAD OF POLICE *with drawn revolvers, led by a grizzly, brutal-faced* CAPTAIN *run into the room. They are followed by* MARGARET *still distractedly clutching the pieces of the plan to her breast.*

CAPTAIN (*pointing to the mask of* DION – *triumphantly*). Got him! He's dead!

MARGARET (*throws herself on her knees, takes the mask and kisses it – heart-brokenly*). Dion! Dion!

Her face hidden in her arms, the mask in her hands above her bowed head, she remains, sobbing with deep, silent grief.

CAPTAIN (*noticing* CYBEL *and* BROWN – *startled*). Hey! Look at this! What're you doin' here? Who's he?

CYBEL. You ought to know. You croaked him!

CAPTAIN (*with a defensive snarl – hastily*). It was Anthony! I saw his mug! This feller's an accomplice, I bet yuh! Serves him right! Who is he? Friend o' yours! Crook! What's his name? Tell me or I'll fix yuh!

CYBEL. Billy.

CAPTAIN. Billy what?

CYBEL. I don't know. He's dying. (*Then suddenly.*) Leave me alone with him and maybe I'll get him to squeal it.

CAPTAIN. Yuh better! I got to have a clean report. I'll give yuh a couple o' minutes.

He motions to the POLICEMEN, *who follow him off left.* CYBEL *takes off her mask and sits down by* BROWN's *head. He makes an effort to raise himself toward her and she helps him, throwing her kimono over his bare body, drawing his head on to her shoulders.*

BROWN (*snuggling against her – gratefully*). The earth is warm.

CYBEL (*soothingly, looking before her like an idol*). Ssshh! Go to sleep, Billy.

BROWN. Yes, Mother. (*Then explainingly.*) It was dark and I couldn't see where I was going and they all picked on me.

CYBEL. I know. You're tired.

BROWN. And when I wake up . . .?

CYBEL. The sun will be rising again.

BROWN. To judge the living and the dead! (*Frightenedly.*) I don't want justice. I want love.

CYBEL. There is only love.

BROWN. Thank you, Mother. (*Then feebly.*) I'm getting sleepy. What's the prayer you taught me – Our Father – ?

CYBEL (*with calm exultance*). Our Father Who Art!

BROWN (*taking her tone – exultantly*). Who art! Who art! (*Suddenly – with ecstasy.*) I know! I have found Him! I hear Him speak!

'Blessed are they that weep, for they shall laugh!' Only he that has wept can laugh! The laughter of Heaven sows earth with a rain of tears, and out of Earth's transfigured birth-pain the laughter of Man returns to bless and play again in innumerable dancing gales of flame upon the knees of God! (*He dies.*)

CYBEL (*gets up and arranges his body on the couch. She bends down and kisses him gently – she straightens up and looks into space – with a profound pain*). Always spring comes again bearing life! Always again! Always, always for ever again! – Spring again! – life again! – summer and autumn and death and peace again! – (*With agonised sorrow.*) – but always, always, love and conception and birth and pain again – spring bearing the intolerable chalice of life again! – (*Then with agonised exultance.*) – bearing the glorious, blazing crown of life again! (*She stands like an idol of Earth, her eyes staring out over the world.*)

MARGARET (*lifting her head adoringly to the mask – triumphant tenderness mingled with her grief*). My lover! My husband! My boy! (*She kisses the mask.*) Goodbye. Thank you for happiness! And you're not dead, sweetheart! You can never die till my heart dies! You will live for ever! You will sleep under my heart! I will feel you stirring in your sleep, for ever under my heart! (*She kisses the mask again. There is a pause.*)

CAPTAIN (*comes just into sight at left and speaks front without looking at them – gruffly*). Well, what's his name?

CYBEL. Man.

CAPTAIN (*taking a grimy notebook and an inch-long pencil from his pocket*). How d'yuh spell it?

Curtain.

EPILOGUE

Scene. Four years later.

The same spot on the same pier as in Prologue on another moonlight night in June. The sound of the waves and of distant dance music.

MARGARET *and her three sons appear from the right. The eldest is now eighteen. All are dressed in the height of correct school elegance. They are all tall, athletic, strong and handsome-looking. They loom up around the slight figure of their mother like protecting giants, giving her a strange aspect of lonely, detached, small femininity. She wears her mask of the proud, indulgent Mother. She has grown appreciably older. Her hair is now a beautiful grey. There is about her manner and voice the sad but contented feeling of one who knows her life-purpose well accomplished but is at the same time a bit empty and comfortless with the finality of it. She is wrapped in a grey cloak.*

ELDEST. Doesn't Bee look beautiful tonight, Mother?

NEXT. Don't you think Mabel's the best dancer in there, Mother?

YOUNGEST. Aw, Alice has them both beat, hasn't she, Mother?

MARGARET (*with a sad little laugh*). Each of you is right. (*Then with strange finality*). Goodbye boys.

BOYS (*surprised*). Goodbye.

MARGARET. It was here on a night just like this your father first – proposed to me. Did you ever know that?

BOYS (*embarrassedly*). No.

MARGARET (*yearningly*). But the nights now are so much colder than they used to be. Think of it, I went in for moonlight-bathing in June when I was a girl. It was so warm and beautiful in those days. I remember the Junes when I was carrying you boys – (*A pause. They fidget uneasily. She asks pleadingly.*) Promise me faithfully never to forget your father!

BOYS (*uncomfortably*). Yes, Mother.

MARGARET (*forcing a joking tone*). But you mustn't waste June on an old woman like me! Go in and dance. (*As they hesitate dutifully.*) Go on. I really want to be alone – with my Junes.

BOYS (*unable to conceal their eagerness*). Yes, Mother. (*They go away.*)

MARGARET (*slowly removes her mask, laying it on the bench, and stares up at the moon with a wistful resigned sweetness*). So long ago! And yet I'm still the same Margaret. It's only our lives that grow old. We *are* where centuries only count as seconds and after a thousand lives our eyes begin to open – (*She looks around her with a rapt smile.*) – and the moon rests in the sea! I want to feel the moon at peace in the sea! I want Dion to leave the sky for me! I want him to sleep in the tides of my heart! (*She slowly takes from under her cloak, from her bosom, as if from her heart, the mask of* DION *as it was at the last and holds it before her face.*) My lover! My husband! My boy! You can never die till my heart dies! You will live for ever! You are sleeping under my heart! I feel you stirring in your sleep, for ever under my heart. (*She kisses him on the lips with a timeless kiss.*)

Curtain.